T0345509

A BOOKSHOP
IN
CHELSEA

Leo and Philippa Bernard: this photograph was taken by a Japanese tourist – it arrived in the post one day from Tokyo.

A BOOKSHOP
IN
CHELSEA

PHILIPPA BERNARD

Unicorn Press

First published in 2023 by
Unicorn Press
60 Bracondale
Norwich NR1 2AS
UK

tradfordhugh@gmail.com
www.unicornpublishing.org

A CIP record of this book can be obtained from the British Library
ISBN 978 1 739164 01 0

Designed by Karen Wilks
Printed in Malta by Gutenberg Press Ltd

*This book is dedicated to my niece Rachel Spence
who first thought of the idea.*

Contents

Acknowledgements

So many people have helped me with this book that I could not name them all. But these in particular I should like to thank: Professor Jack Spence, Rachel Spence, Jonathan Footerman, all the girls who helped in the shop – Venetia, Tina, Juliet, Rohays, Anna, Jane, Rachel 2, Caro, Georgina; members of the antiquarian book trade – Angus O'Neill, Sheila Markham, Barbara Grigor Taylor, Ed Maggs, Amanda Hall and Keith Fletcher were particularly generous with their help; friends in Chelsea – Tony Ashby, Chantal Coady and Ros Roden; David and Julie Loebell; Giles Mandelbrote; and especially at Unicorn Press, Hugh Tempest-Radford.

Foreword

I t all started with the troughs. Each morning, well before the shop officially opened, stout wooden trolleys would be trundled out onto the pavement outside, traps set and baited for unsuspecting passers-by. On the way to work, it was all too easy to be waylaid by interesting and often unusual books, at greatly reduced prices. Giving in to temptation led into the shop, an oasis of calm amid the bustle of rush-hour Chelsea, and to conversation with Leo and Philippa Bernard, who became my friends.

This book offers a portrait of the bookshop at 313 King's Road which Leo and Philippa ran between 1971 and 1999. The shop had large windows, and keen-eyed proprietors, so this is also a view into another world, that of Chelsea in the 1970s and 1980s, when the end of the King's Road furthest from Sloane Square still felt like a neighbourhood, with small shops and many long-term residents.

London has lost many of its bookshops now, particularly those like Chelsea Rare Books, which combined a dependable secondhand stock of books to read, on a wide range of history, literature, biography and travel, with more collectable antiquarian books in handsome bindings. Here is an evocative account, at first hand, of what it was like to run one of those shops at a time when customers paid by cheque (if at all), when stock was selected by judgement and serendipity rather than by algorithm, and questions would be answered by a carefully-chosen library of reference books rather than by Google.

Leo and Philippa made a habit of inspecting their customers as rigorously as they inspected their books and they could be trenchant in summing up both – occasionally before the customers were out of earshot. Philippa's vivid sketches of their clientele, of booksellers and runners, and of those who had simply wandered in, bring to life celebrities and tramps, aristocrats and authors, scholars and students: the interesting, the eccentric and the downright mad.

The shop was not only there to sell books; it also functioned as a kind of salon. To turn these pages is to be reminded of the handsomely furnished shop, of Leo's avuncular welcome and appetite for literary and philosophical debate, of Philippa's curiosity and restless energy, of the ebb and flow of conversation. I can hear it still.

Giles Mandelbrote,
Librarian and Director of Collections,
The Warburg Institute

Introduction

Reminiscing with my family over Christmas lunch, about the happy days at Chelsea Rare Books, we recalled some of the customers and many of the books we had met during the thirty years we were in Chelsea. My niece Rachel, sitting beside me, had worked in the shop for a year or two; she reminded me of some of the lovely girls who helped us and with whom I am still in touch. We spoke of Tess the cocker spaniel, as much a member of staff as any of the girls. We laughed again at the quaint vagaries of the customers, the neighbours and the friends who called in for coffee or a glass of wine.

'That shop was unlike any other,' someone said. 'We mustn't let it be forgotten.' Silence fell on the guests round the table. 'You have to write the story of CRB,' two people said together. Everyone agreed, chattering together as more and more memories came flooding out. 'Do you remember…?' And we did remember. We remembered Juliet, our assistant, whom an Arab wanted to buy. And the MP who bought books to clothe his shelves at a party and brought them back when his guests had gone home. And the Greek for whom we spent thousands of his money on books and furniture for his new home.

Sadly my husband Leo died before this book was written, but he was a happy man. Not many men or women love every moment of their working day, looking forward on Sunday night to going back to work on Monday morning. So here it is, the story of the shop 'unlike any other'. It won't be forgotten.

Philippa Bernard
June, 2023

CHAPTER I

In the Beginning

After breakfast one spring morning in 1971, Leo was reading *The Times*. He called to me, 'Come and look at this.' I left the washing up and leaned over his shoulder. He pointed to a few lines in the Personal Column. The short advertisement read: *Antiquarian Bookshop for sale in Chelsea. Large stock included. Telephone for an appointment to view.*

An appointment was duly arranged and we drove down to the King's Road in our old Ford Escort. Parking meters had only been in use in Chelsea for a few years and we found a free space in Paultons Square and walked to the shop near the corner of Beaufort Street, opposite the Blue Bird Café. That Grade II listed building had been the former Blue Bird Garage, associated with Sir Malcom Campbell.

Leo found the shop – Chelsea Rare Books (often known as CRB) – irresistible. We had married in 1953, and had dreamed for some years of owning a bookshop. We had no children, had paid off the mortgage on our house in north London and Leo hated his work in the small advertising agency which he owned with a friend. The shop was double-fronted, with a staircase at the back leading down to a basement full of rubbish. Shelved from floor to ceiling, all full of books, the shop was a curiously attractive

cross between a gentleman's library and a modern book emporium. The furniture consisted of two tables, one octagonal mahogany and the other square heavy oak, together with a large knee-hole desk and a tall, elegant glass-fronted bookcase. The elderly dark green carpet was worn in places. There were two or three mahogany dining chairs for customers to relax in while they examined the books.

The owners of the shop, Robin Greer and his wife, showed us round, clearly very knowledgeable about the stock and the antiquarian book trade, of which we Bernards knew absolutely nothing. Time flew by as customers came and went. Soon it was six o'clock – time to close the shop. A card notice – one corner missing – hanging on the door, was turned round to read CLOSED from the outside. Leo was reluctant to leave and the Greers insisted on opening a bottle of wine once the door was locked.

'Let's go over the road and have something to eat,' I suggested. One of the many good little restaurants in that part of Chelsea was La Casserole, owned by a big friendly Australian chef, Tom, one of the gay community in King's Road at that time. Later we came to know him well. By the end of the evening we had agreed to buy the shop.

There was much to do. The Greers wanted £16,000 for the stock, furnishings and fittings, including the remaining lease of some 25 years. The rent was high for those days (£700 p.a.) and the business rates, even for a prime site in an expensive part of London, seemed extortionate. However, Leo's agency was under offer to a large advertising conglomerate, mainly because of one important client; and an elderly lady who had known him since childhood, and who had had the good fortune to marry three consecutive millionaires, wanted to put some money in. Leo's accountant, Lewis Golden, another good friend, strongly advised us against doing anything so rash as to go into an enterprise we knew nothing about, so we ignored him, accepted the elderly lady's offer of help, and set matters in hand.

Born in 1926, Leo grew up in Hampstead and was educated at University College School. A voracious reader, he had always loved books, especially English Literature, Philosophy and Religion; after school he had taken a course at the London School of Printing. In spite of being quietly introspective, he enjoyed sport, playing rugby for his school (when his nose was broken in a tackle by a Metropolitan Police team) and was a keen Arsenal supporter. When war broke out in 1939 he was anxious to join up but was much too young. Nevertheless in 1942, still under age, he went into the Navy Recruiting Office in Finchley Road. He was found to be colour blind and was turned down. As he was leaving, a burly Royal Marine sergeant stuck out his arm. 'Where do you think you're going?' Five minutes later he was in the Royal Marines and soon on his way to RM headquarters in Deal. He went over to France on D-Day, landing on Sword Beach and came through the war unscathed.

I had been educated at Berkhamsted School for Girls, hated it in spite of receiving an excellent education, and refused to try for university. Instead I took a bi-lingual secretarial course at the French Lycée in London, and then worked in the French Section of the BBC until at the age of twenty, I left to marry Leo. I had various part-time jobs in publishing, and when we bought the house in North London I spent as much time as possible in our new garden. I too was a great reader, though my tastes turned more to history and biography.

In 1971 the Open University began its first courses. When news appeared in the press, announcing the foundation of a new form of learning, I was very intrigued. I had turned down the opportunity to go to university after school but the offer of a second chance with the 'University of the Air', as it was first called, seemed too good to be true. Using modern technology, face to face tutorials and a great deal of hard work at home, I thought it would be just right for me and I signed on. I opted for as many of the humanities courses as I could. My first venture into an intensive world of higher education coincided almost exactly with our purchase of the shop.

Friends tried to persuade us to leave the much-loved house in Totteridge and find a home in Chelsea. But we knew we could never find a similar three-bedroomed house with a large garden on our budget so we decided to stay where we were and commute by car, sharing the driving and doing our best to avoid the rush hours.

We opened a new bank account at Barclays across the road in Chelsea, with both our signatures on cheques. The Bank Manager interviewed us personally and we found him a great help when we needed advice. In those days a Bank Manager took an interest in all his customers. In fact once or twice a year he and Leo would go out to lunch, mainly to talk about cricket – I was never invited!

Terrified by our total lack of bookselling experience, we were fortunate to inherit with the shop a delightful part-time assistant. Venetia was introduced to her new employers and was happy to continue working three days a week. Robin Greer, too, said he would come in for a while to ensure a smooth handover. All was set for the new adventure.

Chapter 2

The Shop is Open

Chelsea Rare Books opened under new management on September 20th 1971. Terrified that we might forget the keys, or have an accident on the way, we arrived at 313 King's Road, at 8.30, in spite of the fact that the notice on the door read 'Opening Hours: MONDAY TO SATURDAY, 10 AM TO 6 PM.' There was no-one about and most of the other shops in King's Road were still closed. The first thing to do, obviously, was to put the kettle on. At the back of the shop was a small cloakroom, with a sink and lavatory, and a cupboard which held a few cracked cups and saucers, a half bottle of milk and some questionable tea and coffee packs. The milk was off. But the kettle worked from a plug by the desk, and the little general shop across the road was open. I walked over to buy milk and introduced myself to the Pakistani owners, also husband and wife, who became good friends. Leo wandered round our shop, bemused; was this going to be the biggest mistake of his life?

Half-an-hour later Venetia arrived, and suddenly anything seemed possible. She was full of smiles and confidence. 'I'll put the troughs out', she said. 'No, let me do it,' Leo insisted. Never the most nimble fingered, he seemed unable to manage the simple hook and eye fixture at the back of the boxes to attach them to the windowsills outside the shop. After a wink from me,

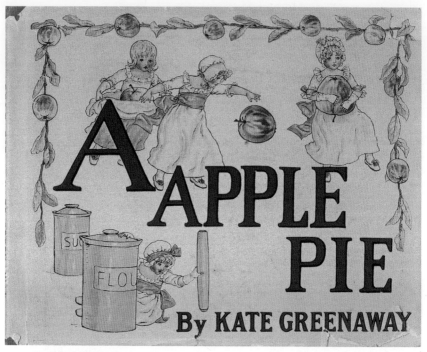

Kate Greenway, ABC

Venetia went to help. 'You'll soon get used to it,' she said soothingly. As they turned to go in, an elderly man took a book from the trough. 'Can I take this please?' He handed over a 50p piece – Leo had made his first sale.

It soon became clear that although there were many people visiting the shop, that did not mean many people bought books. The door was always open for browsers, some who just wanted to look round, others who asked for a particular book, or perhaps 'anything on cricket', or a Charles Dickens first edition. All the books were priced in pencil on the flyleaf so there were no problems about what to charge. Venetia seemed to be able to answer any question put to her, knew the stock and was unfailingly cheerful even in the face of the most irritating visitors. An important feature of the book stock was early children's books, a somewhat specialised field. I was well versed in classic children's stories and I could recite by heart much of A.A. Milne's best children's verse, including *King John Was Not a Good Man* and *The*

Philippa at her desk with Tess below

King's Breakfast, but knew little of the great children's book illustrators, and nothing at all of the prices these early editions were fetching. In fact our first real sale was to a young father building up a library for his little girl, then only a few months old. He asked for anything illustrated by Kate Greenaway. Venetia opened the glass bookcase and took out a beautiful copy of *A Apple Pie*, Greenaway's first alphabet book, with its charming cover of little girls in mob caps chasing apples. The customer snapped it up, in spite of what seemed to me a ridiculous price. This was before the advent of credit cards so the customer wrote out a cheque and smilingly handed it over to Venetia. 'Would you like us to let you know of anything else like this we may get in?' she asked. 'Oh yes please. Thank you so much.' As he left the shop, we felt we had learned the lesson of a lifetime.

Leo at his desk

We made few alterations to the layout of the shop at the beginning, except to make it a little more convenient for ourselves. The counter, a heavy wooden structure with a smooth brown surface – lino perhaps – was in the centre of the shop and fixed to the floor. About a metre wide by two metres long, it was ideal for packing books, writing or typing and generally putting things down on. The front, a solid piece of board facing the windows, was useful for displaying notices or posters, and at the back underneath was deep shelving for paper bags, wrapping materials, the cashbox (we had no till but used the same battered wooden cigar box for some thirty years) and other things such as handbags, sandwiches for lunch and personal belongings, including spare shoes, spectacles, rain hats etc. There was also a high stool to rest our often weary limbs. From this vantage point you could see the street and keep an eye on the whole shop.

I had a small desk near the window, from which I could watch visitors. If they needed help they stopped at my desk; if they just wanted to browse they could walk past me into the shop and look along the shelves.

2. The Shop is Open

Leo sat behind his mahogany leather-topped desk at the back of the shop, except when he was sorting books, pricing, serving, or out on business. Behind him were a couple of shelves containing our reference books. Before computers the most important of these was a set of *Book Auction Records*. Published every year, this was a priced and annotated annual record of international book auctions. It was important to know what price copies of any important book had sold for previously and the comprehensive information for every entry enabled us to check that the copies we held were correct in every detail.

There were many other sets of reference books: bibliographies of all kinds, such as on books on angling or the Far East, or by a single author, on printing or bookbinding. We found a considerable number of these on the shelves when we arrived but needed to buy more as our experience widened. They were a valuable source of knowledge about the world of books, particularly for novices at the game. Now of course most of what booksellers need to know is online, but when we took over CRB, and for many years after, we needed extensive volumes of bibliographic material: one in French was the *Dictionnaire Bibliographique de Livres Rares*, of 1860, by Jacques Brunet, in six volumes. We also had William Lowndes' *The Bibliographer's Manual of English Literature* – the first systematic work of the kind – published in four volumes in 1834. Halkett and Laing's *Dictionary of Anonymous and Pseudonymous English Literature* was a very useful four-volume set for when the author was not mentioned in the book.

———•+•———

The shop was run entirely by Leo and me, with the help of one part-time assistant. We did everything ourselves: cleaning, tidying, keeping the accounts, banking, writing letters, compiling catalogues. We did also have the assistance of our friend Lewis, the accountant, who in spite of his disapproval to begin with, loved the shop and bought books from us from time to time. He took it upon himself to instruct me in the art of double-entry bookkeeping. I never told him I had previously done a bookkeeping course at secretarial college. When I queried his instructions, puzzled by his expert advice, he said, 'A child of five could understand that!' But he was very patient and I soon adapted his commercial teachings to the very simple method we used. There were no computers at that stage, though we did have a very simple adding machine, and a portable typewriter. Later I did learn to use a computer, an early Amstrad, though we never got as far as mobile phones. Leo refused to accept the use of computers or the web – 'It'll never last,' he said!

One field where we did have to employ a professional was repairing and binding books. We had inherited from Robin Greer a very skilled bookbinder called Anthony Wessely. He lived near Ascot but came into town frequently to visit his customers in the book trade, and we entrusted to him some valuable books which needed repair or even a complete rebind. He was a master at retaining as much of the original bindings as he could, incorporating new material where necessary and using beautiful calligraphy for the gilt lettering on the covers and spines.

Later we got to know a young bookbinder who had just finished his training at the Camberwell School of Art. Red-haired Rob Shepherd later became one of the leading binders in England. He bought out Sangorski and Sutcliffe, perhaps the oldest bookbinders in the world, and played an important part in the Antiquarian Booksellers Association. Just before the King's Coronation, it was announced that the new Bible traditionally used by the monarch to swear his coronation oath, and presented to him afterwards, had been specially bound by Shepherd, Sangorski and Sutcliffe. Sadly Rob died of cancer in 2022.

Although credit cards were coming into use, it took some time for us to link in to Barclaycard. Diners Club were the first to attract the public, followed by American Express. Many high street shops were not too keen on American Express – they charged the retailer more for the privilege of credit – but the usual method of payment then was cash or cheque. Names and addresses were always added on the back of a cheque and if a large sum was

Shepherds Bookbinders

involved and we didn't know the customer well, we insisted the cheque clear before the books were taken away. We usually offered to post or deliver the purchase at our expense. The card machines were heavy and awkward and we kept them under the counter. We had very few problems with bouncing cheques or refused cards.

It was important for us to learn the technology of book making. Leo was quite knowledgeable from his days at the London School of Printing, but I didn't know the difference between folio, quarto or octavo, what an endpaper was, or how to distinguish between calf and Morocco. Perhaps the most useful book I ever acquired was John Carter's *ABC for Book Collectors*. This easily-read reference work told the reader almost everything he needed to know about how to describe a book, what the technical terms relating to book making were and much about the art of putting together a beautiful book.

We were learning all the time. Every book was different and modern methods of bookbinding, typography and of course the subjects of the books were

Fore-edge painting

changing rapidly as communication facilities and electronic mechanisms came into being. I remember the first time I met a fore-edge painting on a book. This is a painting executed when the fore-edge of a book is fanned back to allow the artist to paint a delicate picture, often related to the book's contents, along the trimmed edge of the pages. When the pages are restored to their former position, the picture becomes invisible. An even rarer possession is a double fore-edge, when the pages can be fanned back in either direction with a painting on each. On one occasion we bought such a treasure inexpensively at auction from a box of books, because no one had noticed the presence of the painting on the edge of the closed book.

The stock of books in the shop when we took over was very varied. There were few subjects excluded, other than those we didn't care to have. In this category came books on the occult, murder stories (other than classics such as Sherlock Holmes or Agatha Christie first editions) and biographies by 'footballers' wives' – a term used by some booksellers to indicate almost unsaleable trash. If they happened to come along, we could always use these in the outside troughs.

Because of our own interests we tended to buy valuable books on literature, some important political biographies and histories, sporting books, particularly field sports, and books on travel. This was a vital field, as early

David Roberts, Syria

books on, say, the Middle East, America, East Africa or Southern Asia were much sought after. These, often with magnificent contemporary illustrations, fetched very good prices, many running into four figures or even more. These encouraged foreign book buyers, both private and trade, to visit us whenever they were in London, sure that they would find some worthwhile purchases. We soon got to know which writers and travellers attracted our customers: David Roberts' magnificent views of Syria and the Arab countries were greatly sought after. So was Thomas and William Daniells' great work on India, *Oriental Scenery*, with beautiful aquatints, and any by James Cook on Australia. More modern authors such as Patrick Leigh Fermor and Freya Stark were very popular.

But gradually we expanded the range of books, choosing subjects we hadn't met before: early cookery, gardening, fine printing and a few classics. We found that as we included a wider field, so our customer range extended too, and there were few buyers we were unable to satisfy.

Battersea Old Bridge: etching by Walter Burgess.

As we settled into a new life and a new environment, we found that exploring Chelsea was a fascinating background to the shop itself. Our corner of the King's Road was sited on what had been the garden of Sir Thomas More's house. Thinking back to *A Man for All Seasons* I found myself imagining the area as it had been in his time. The mulberry trees that he planted are still there, dropping their berries as they ripen and covering the ground beneath them with slippery black juice.

Chelsea was at one time the market garden for London. Its fertile river banks provided much of the fruit and vegetables for the city, the produce ferried down river when the Thames was the principal highway for the capital. The village was once called the 'village of palaces', with splendid mansions, such as that owned by Henry VIII – who built the Manor House in Cheyne Walk as a present for his sixth wife, Katherine Parr – and those of the Duke of Norfolk and the Earl of Shrewsbury. Hans Sloane, whose vast collection of antiquities formed the nucleus of the British Museum, was the last to live in the old Manor House before it was demolished.

2. The Shop is Open

Chelsea Old Church, just round the corner from the shop, was first built in the twelfth century and its familiar square tower – not now the original – appeared often in the drawings and paintings we sold in the shop, as did the old wooden Battersea Bridge and the Rotunda which was the focal point of the Ranelagh Pleasure Gardens, now the site of the annual Chelsea Flower Show.

Crosby Hall reminded me of the old medieval buildings in the city – it had been moved in 1910 to the Chelsea riverside from its original site in Bishopsgate. Later I became so absorbed in Chelsea's history that I wrote a small book for those who wanted to know more, and often asked us for information: *A Visitor's Guide to Chelsea*, which came out in 1983 and was reprinted in 1992.

When we first arrived there were about twelve booksellers in the King's Road, including the splendid and – it is to be hoped – everlasting John Sandoe, the small shop beside Peter Jones, selling new books and unrivalled in its service to customers. Other new book shops that came along later were a branch of Waterstones, and Daunts in Fulham Road. There were several second-hand bookshops in the two antique markets, Antiquarius and the Chelsea Antique Market. Peter and Adrian Harrington operated from there – they are now in the Fulham Road. Further down on the 'bend' was – and still is – World's End Bookshop.

Another bookseller operated from his beautiful house in Park Walk. Robin de Beaumont was a man of grace and distinction. After Cambridge, where he studied architecture and started collecting books, Robin had been in the Air Force and then started the antiquarian book department of Stanley Gibbons, the stamp company. His principal field of collecting was Victorian illustrated books. So important was the collection that he eventually presented it to the British Museum. Robin was to be seen at every book fair; he was known to booklovers across the world, and was liked and respected by them all.

Sadly he died in the spring of 2023. His friends and family gathered after the funeral at the Chelsea Arts Club, where the talk, remembering Robin, was of books and book collecting.

CHAPTER 3

Troughs and Trollies

The troughs outside the shop containing cheap books, all under £1, were inherited from Robin Greer. They resembled the stalls of the bouquinistes along the Seine in Paris, giving an air of bohemian trade, very suitable for Chelsea. They were strong wooden trays with sturdy metal legs on casters and could be attached to the shop windowsills. We put them out as soon as we arrived in the mornings and took them in at night. On one occasion we forgot and left them out all night. In the morning we found some cash on the doormat and gaps in the boxes. Some customers were more honest than others. We also had a rather smart black and white striped blind to roll down if it rained or was too hot. Heavy rain during the night meant that water gathered in the folds of the blind and letting it down in the morning meant a flood sloshed down on to the pavement and on to any unwary passer-by.

Another legacy from Robin was a heavy-duty sack trolley with pneumatic tyres for transporting books. It was easy to push along but very strong, and could take three wine-box size cartons, very useful at book fairs or for collecting large purchases. Unused to such onerous work it took us both some time to get used to lugging about those heavy boxes, but we soon acquired muscles we didn't know we had, and even now in ripe old age I

Street view of the shop.

can carry far greater weights than most of my contemporaries. When we eventually left the shop we took the trolley home for use in the garden, until after more than fifty years' use it fell apart under a heavy flowerpot.

We also inherited an excellent stepladder to reach the higher shelves. This too was on casters and could be rolled along the floor when needed. It was safe enough for even a child to climb on, which happened frequently. More elegant, but equally useful, were spiral library steps, made of mahogany with leather covers to the steps and a pole at the side to hang on to.

We noticed from time to time the regular visits to the troughs from an old, shabby, somewhat disreputable-looking tramp, who wore a medallion in the centre of his forehead. He was a big man, slightly stooped, with long hair and a shaggy beard. He always carried a shapeless bag over his shoulder and shuffled along the pavement in dirty ragged shoes. As soon as he saw him, Leo would rush out of the shop and shoo him away. One day, alone in the shop,

The glass cabinet.

I saw the tramp take a book from the trough and after a quick look round, walk away with it. A few days later it happened again. We discussed what we should do. It was hardly a case for the police – nothing in the troughs was priced at more than a pound, and there was no resale value in the books, so the man was clearly a reader. Perhaps he was a genius in disguise, an author, unable to afford the research materials he needed? We made a decision.

The next time we saw him Leo went outside. 'Good morning, friend,' he said to the 'customer', who had a book in his hand. 'I was going to put it back, honest, guvnor,' said the thief. 'Let's have an agreement,' Leo said sternly. 'You can steal one book a week but no more. If I catch you taking any others, I'll call the police. Understood?' The tramp touched his non-existent cap and shambled off. After that he would take his chosen book, hold it up as he gave us a wave, and be on his way.

The troughs were a very useful source of loose change. The purchases were almost always paid for in cash, and we put the money in the old cigar box. Without entering anything in the accounts, we took coins, or sometimes notes, out for petty cash, to pay for refreshments and other minor shopping – Leo used to say that he thought it was 'unpatriotic to trouble the tax-man'. For larger sales in cash we took some home, declared most and looked on the rest as 'housekeeping'. As we didn't pay ourselves a regular salary, this seemed only fair. I cannot remember ever drawing out cash to pay for household running costs or weekly shopping.

We were fussy about the way we transported books. Using the trolley where possible, cardboard boxes were a vital part of the shop 'furniture'. The best boxes were strong 12-bottle wine cartons. They were made to be strong yet portable. Friends along the road kept boxes for us, knowing exactly what we considered suitable. We slotted one open box into another as the sizes varied, never flattening them as other shopkeepers did. When they were full of books the four flaps could be interleaved to keep the books safe. Packing the books in was an art in itself. It was usually possible to get four octavo volumes in one layer. They had to lie flat – Leo's wrath came down on anyone who dared to pack books on spines or fore-edges, and great care was taken of dust-wrappers, very important, particularly in the case of modern first editions.

After a few years in the shop, when we were more familiar with the book trade and those who worked in it, we felt the need to branch out a little. Most booksellers participated in monthly Book Fairs held all over the country, some under the auspices of the Provincial Booksellers Fairs Association, and a few held yearly in the bigger cities and run by the Antiquarian Booksellers Association. Robin Greer had been a member of the ABA, but if a shop changed hands the new owners had to reapply to join. This we were determined to do once the stipulated five years ownership was up.

The ABA is the senior trade body in the British Isles for dealers in antiquarian and rare books, manuscripts and allied materials. Founded in 1906 and the oldest organisation of its kind in the world, the Antiquarian Booksellers Association represents the interests of over 230 member businesses, by creating a high standard of business ethics and professional standards. The British Association was a leading member of ILAB, the International League of Antiquarian Booksellers, and concerned itself with the proper running and conduct of the trade.

We put in our application for membership, sponsored by Robin Greer himself and by one of the leading bookshops in the world, Maggs Bros. of Berkeley Square. John Maggs, then head of the firm, was pleased to help. He was the fourth generation of Maggses to run the business. His son Edward is now in charge. Many are the wonderful stories about the firm. In 1916 Maggs Bros bought the penis of Napoleon Bonaparte from the descendants of Abbé Ange Paul Vignali, who had given the last rites and surreptitiously cut off the member in question after the Emperor died. Vignali apparently brought it to Corsica, and died in a vendetta in 1828. It was passed on to his sister, who at her death passed it on to her son. In 1924, the desiccated item was sold to a Dr. A. S. Rosenbach, who mounted it in a case of blue morocco and velvet. In 1927, it was exhibited at the Museum of French Art.

Chelsea Rare Books at a book fair.

We achieved membership of the ABA in due course and looked forward to our first important Book Fair. Originally the ABA Book Fairs had been held at the offices of the National Book League in Albemarle Street, but the organisation grew and bigger premises were needed. The event moved to hotels, until it finally took over Olympia. It was not always easy to get a stall at the important book fairs. Competition was quite fierce and space was limited. The first time we applied, in 1981 – the Fair was at the Marriott Hotel in Duke Street – we were turned down but were put on the waiting list. Two days before the fair was due to start Leo said he didn't feel too well – pains in his chest, feeling clammy, a bit wobbly – I said we should go across to St Stephens Hospital, in the Fulham Road. He told me not to fuss and had a cup of coffee. While he was occupied I went out and fetched the car. We drove round to the hospital and went into the small waiting room. Leo lit a cigarette and a nurse came over. She snatched the cigarette out of his mouth – it was the last one he ever smoked. Someone grabbed a wheelchair and pushed him into it. He was wheeled away while I filled in a form. 'Can I stay?' I asked mildly. 'No, phone us in an hour. Let us do our job!'

I drove back to the shop, bewildered and upset. It turned out not to be too serious but it was a warning of possible heart problems in the future. The hospital kept Leo in overnight and let him out the next day. Meanwhile I had another difficulty to deal with. While I was out a phone message asked us to ring the ABA. When I did so I was faced with an offer to do the fair after all – someone had fallen out and there was a stand free. I rushed back to the hospital and consulted with Leo. 'You can't do it yourself,' he said. 'Yes, I can,' I insisted. And I did, with the help of several of our girls and the generous advice of fellow booksellers. We didn't make a fortune, but we held our own and I was able to report back to Leo that our first ABA Fair had not been a disaster.

After that we exhibited at the London ABA Fair each year, enjoying the atmosphere and the opportunity to meet other booksellers from across the world. One year Leo was appointed Chairman of the Book Fair Committee. The Fair was opened each year by a distinguished personality, ranging from royalty to the worlds of entertainment or bookselling. When it was Leo's turn to head the Committee the opener was Sir Kenneth Baker, then Minister of State for Education.

We participated in many Fairs out of London. One particularly memorable occasion was the Edinburgh Fair, when the Scottish Branch of the ABA entertained us royally, with Haggis and Neeps, accompanied by more whisky than I knew existed. I don't like whisky but Leo took his share. He didn't appear the worse for wear, but did try to walk through a glass door which was closed at the time. No damage was done to him or the door.

We were regularly represented at the Chelsea Fair, on home territory at the Town Hall in King's Road, where many of our customers came to visit us. Other venues were Bath, Brighton, York, Oxford and Cambridge – always a good excuse to get out of town for a few days, usually to somewhere of historic interest, where we were sure to be welcomed and handsomely entertained. Usually the booksellers of the town where the Fair was to be held put on visits, exhibitions or events of interest, with a formal dinner and plenty of food and drink throughout the Fair.

Some of these fairs were under the auspices of the PBFA (the Provincial Booksellers Fairs Association). There was a certain rivalry between the two organisations, some booksellers belonging to both, others to none at all, though only members could exhibit. Both tried to help their members where they could, upheld standards and if necessary intervened in disputes between the trade and the public. The ABA had a Press Officer to publicise bookselling matters of general interest, and to get as much coverage as possible for the Fairs and for unusual events in the bookselling world.

CHAPTER 4

Leo's Girls

From the moment we bought the shop, when Venetia welcomed us so warmly, we were fortunate to employ, part-time, a series of delightful girls. When each felt it time to move on, for marriage, moving house, babies or other reasons, she was usually able to find us a friend, just as suitable, to take her place. As the babies arrived more frequently, Leo began to write little poems for their birthdays, rather along the lines of A.A. Milne's in *When We Were Very Young*, which of course their mothers loved.

For Tina's son Charles:
Time for sunshine, shirtsleeves, cricket,
Strawberries and cream for tea,
Charles in great form at the wicket –
And the scoreboard says 'He's THREE!'

And Juliet's daughter Isabelle:
Isabelle's three – let's have a spree, Everyone is invited to tea!
Now who can bake a birthday cake? Juliet if she's awake.
Games, too, and dancing, skipping and prancing,
Nannies retreating, children advancing.
Presents and prizes, funny disguises

All kinds of marvellous birthday surprises.
And who's 'Belle of the Ball', no doubt at all,
Who should that be but the girl that we call
IS-A-BELLE!!

And Anna's son Patrick:
P ut two candles on the cake
A nd icing too, for heaven's sake.
T ell the town, a party's planned
R eady? – right, strike up the band!
I t's time for a big birthday cheer
C ome on, now, March the Ninth is here,
K ind thoughts, then, for another year.

Without exception we found the girls were friends for ever. Now, some fifty years on, each is still in touch. There have been Christmas cards each year, meeting up for tea or lunch, and though most are grandmothers they all seem to look on their days at CRB with great affection.

Anna

Anna was one of the four daughters of a Scottish Baron, red-haired and with a lively charm. She was an artist, mostly in watercolours, and a friend of several of our other 'girls'. When we went to America on a buying trip/holiday we left her in charge of the shop, accompanied by a friend Sam, and didn't enquire too closely what they got up to while we were away.

Rohays

Rohays – the name, I think, is Gaelic – came to us in 1979, after her predecessor left after a short while to have a baby. Rohays was an attractive light-hearted girl, with family connections going back to the Romanovs and Alexander Pushkin, the Werners of

Luton Hoo and, when she married, the, Galitzines. We were invited to her wedding at Dunkeld Cathedral, not far from her family home at Pitlochry in Scotland. In the shop she was popular with the customers and we could leave her alone with no concerns for either her welfare or that of the shop. She came to Aldeburgh with us on more than one occasion. Sadly she has recently passed away.

Tina

Her real name is Katrina and she too had strong Scottish connections. Her father, Sir Charles Troughton, had been a Director of W.H. Smith and became Chairman of the British Council. After her marriage to William, of the Carnegie family, they took a house in Lamont Road, a stone's throw away from the shop. Tina was introduced to us by Rohays and took over in 1980. She is very likeable, and was a most capable assistant, with a strong commercial sense. We always knew that if we were away from the shop, at Aldeburgh perhaps or on a buying trip, CRB was left in good hands. This stood her in good stead when she eventually moved to Scotland and very successfully took over her mother's shop in Ullapool. Two of her four children were born while we had the shop, but after a very short while she returned to work, and we were always pleased to have her back. She, like all his 'girls', understood Leo well – she said there were 'days when one knew to get on with stuff and not to disturb or distract!'

Juliet

Juliet was working at an infant school in The Vale across the road from the shop, often passing by and wishing she could work there. Finally she summoned up the courage to come inside to see if there might be a vacancy. She chatted to us easily and we found her to be just the sort of assistant for us. But we were well suited at that moment and couldn't offer her any work. Not long after we found that our present helper wanted – very reluctantly – to leave. She had been engaged to be married and the wedding was approaching, after which she and her new husband would be leaving London. So we got back to Juliet who was delighted to be offered the post, starting as soon as her present school term ended.

Bright and always cheerful, she was just right for the job. She told us that her mother was a lady-in-waiting to the Queen, in fact had been in attendance at the time the former Princess Elizabeth had succeeded to the throne. Some of the stories about the shop Juliet passed on to her mother, who in turn entertained her employer with them! Apparently Her Majesty was very interested in what her ordinary subjects were up to. But Juliet was easy to be with, and the customers loved her. Our friendly neighbourhood policeman, who called in regularly 'to see how you're doing' but really for his statutory cup of tea and to rest his feet, was quite upset if she wasn' t there. 'Where's the girl with the green eyes?' he wanted to know.

Another customer, a Middle Eastern gentleman, was also very enamoured with Juliet. On one occasion she agreed to deliver his purchases to his beautiful home in Eaton Square. He offered to buy her for a handsome price and take her back to his home somewhere in Arabia. She refused his offer and came back, somewhat flustered, to the shop.

Chelsea at that time was the centre of modern youth, and visitors of all shapes and sizes drifted into the shop. Juliet was alone one afternoon when a slightly scruffy figure, with a strong Cockney accent came in. She eyed him rather suspiciously as he wandered round, and when he asked her to open the locked cabinet, she felt very nervous indeed. He took out several leather-bound volumes, some early English poetry, an expensive book on China, and one or two others on cricket, amounting to a good sum of money. If he paid by cheque, she thought, how could she confirm the validity of his bank account? However, to her relief, he took out a credit card in the name of C. Watts. She did not recognise him or the name on the card. She phoned through the details to the card company and to her horror it was refused. However, she was asked to put the customer on the line, Mr. Watts confirmed his identity and all was well. He asked her to pack up the books so that he could collect them later. Charlie Watts, of the Rolling Stones, was a quiet, pleasant customer, with none of the egocentric arrogance of some other pop artists. He became a good customer, well-read and of formidable intelligence. On one occasion he asked for a book on early African exploration as a birthday present for Mick Jagger. We found the right answer even though it cost little short of a four-figure sum. Charlie's daughter Serafina helped us out in the shop occasionally on a Saturday morning.

Juliet was engaged to a general's son, and shortly after coming to us was married in the Queen's Chapel at St James's Palace. She came back to us after the honeymoon and stayed for some time, even after she became pregnant. She so loved the shop that she determined to return after the baby was born. She did so, but the first day back we found her in tears. 'I want my baby,' she sobbed. So we sent her home, but kept up our friendship, even though she is now a grandmother.

Caro

Caro is a slim attractive girl (once photographed by Cecil Beaton) who had been an art student at the Camberwell School of Art. She was always to be found with her nose in a book. On one occasion we left her alone in the shop, and on our return found her lying down on the floor, head in a book, unaware that several customers were waiting to be served. Luckily our stock had remained intact while Caro took 'time out'. She later married Rodolphe d'Erlanger, and they called their second son Leo as a tribute to Chelsea Rare Books.

Jane

Jane came to us by a different route. I think she was the only assistant with a university degree, apart from my niece Rachel Spence. After university she wanted to work in an art gallery and wandered down the King's Road looking for a job. No-one seemed interested and by the time she reached us she was tired and depressed. She fell in love with the shop as soon as she saw it. She and I talked and she cheered up. She told me that she came from Amersham where I had lived for a large part of my life, and that she had gone to the same school. We asked if she was interested in working in a bookshop instead of a gallery and she jumped at the chance. Leo wrote to her offering her the job. Part of his rather formal letter reads: 'As regards the scope of your work, I think it is sufficient to say that we would like you to become involved in virtually all of our activities: buying – privately, at sales, and in the trade; selling – in the shop, by catalogue and by individual offers; and taking a share of general administration.' Quite a proposal for someone who had never worked in a bookshop in her life.

Rachel 1

Rachel Spence, my niece, had known the shop almost from the time we bought it. Her father was a Professor of Politics, now retired, and Rachel was brought up in an academic atmosphere, in a world of books. She helped out from time to time as a schoolgirl, and after university came to us on a more permanent basis. She loved the shop, enjoyed book fairs and was soon entrusted with buying at auction. She stayed with us for about three years, leaving to take up a post at Selfridges, working on their catalogues, then decided to go freelance, writing travel articles and then specialising in art. She is now an Arts Correspondent for the *Financial Times*.

Sophie

Sophie was the sister of Angus, formerly a bookseller's runner. She was a great reader and a considerable artist. She lived in Oxford but commuted daily by means of the Oxford Tube, a regular coach service. She was familiar with the book trade because of her brother. After a year or so with us she took a holiday in France with her mother Elspeth, staying in the little village of Montcuq near Cahors in south-western France. On her return she told us that she would be leaving us shortly, as she and her mother, known to the family and friends as The Bat (we never found out why) had bought an old chemist's shop in the village to turn into a bookshop. Elspeth was a professional pianist and a fine artist. We later visited them and had several happy holidays there, staying in their flat over the shop. Sophie married a French restaurateur helping him run his restaurant nearby as well as the bookshop.

Rachel 2

Another assistant (blonde, as most of them were) was also Rachel. We distinguished them by number, Rachel 1 and Rachel 2. She joined us in 1993, lived in Battersea and often walked to work through the Park with her rough-haired Jack Russell, Lucca, who behaved immaculately in the shop. Our cocker spaniel Tess had gone by then so there was no competition and Leo would take Lucca for walks round the square or down to the river. Rachel married John, a tree surgeon, the following year and inevitably we lost her when the babies started arriving.

Georgie

Our very last assistant was Georgina (Georgie). The decision to give up the shop had already been made, though we wanted to stay on for another month or two to tie up loose ends and give ourselves a chance to think about the future. A bright Chelsea girl came into the shop and said she had heard we were looking for some help in the shop. Where she got that idea from I don't know. She was not a friend of any of our previous girls, but as she lived locally perhaps the word was about that we had no help at that time. We explained the situation to her and she accepted that if we did take her on it would be for a very limited time. She explained that she was a dancer, though she had no work at the moment, that her father was a writer and she had some experience of working in a shop though not a bookshop. Then she told us that she had been on drugs for a long time but had gone into rehab and had been clean for a year. This was something of a facer, but she was very honest about it, had a charming manner, was clearly intelligent and we liked her. We told her to come back in the morning when we had had an opportunity to think it over.

We decided to take a chance and offered her the job, on the understanding that it could not last very long. She lived on her father's houseboat moored near Battersea Bridge and we had no regrets. She had a friendly personality, was good with customers and well read. Two days later her parents came into the shop while she was not there and thanked us for putting our trust in her and giving her a chance. She turned out to be well worth that trust; we let her buy for us at auction and she never let us down. When we did leave she explained that she wanted to go to the States and take up her dancing career again. We found her a job with a bookshop in Los Angeles.

About two years later I had a letter from her father telling me that in America she had mixed with the wrong crowd, gone back to her old ways and had taken her own life. We felt that had we been able to keep her on at the shop it would never have happened.

We were often known in the trade (and outside it) for the girls who helped in the shop. Not only were they decorative, intelligent and charming, but they knew the stock, clearly loved the shop and the customers, and were a great asset in every respect.

CHAPTER 5

King's Road Neighbours

When we first arrived in Chelsea the area was one of the great centres of modern young society. Another was of course Carnaby Street, off Regent Street. But King's Road offered more space and easy access, with plenty of cheap eating places and constantly changing shops, boutiques and intriguing corners, always with the chance of meeting famous faces. Drop-head cars in the latest designs and colours would sweep down, often stopping in the middle of the road to disgorge flamboyant passengers. We were told of one, to be seen on a Saturday afternoon, containing a charming lion cub called Christian. Two young Australians had bought him for 250 guineas at Harrods – in the days when they sold exotic animals – and took him to visit friends in the area. They wrote a book about him, *A Lion Called Christian*. Soon he grew too big and was released into the wild in Kenya. When his owner later visited him on the reservation, Christian knew him immediately and they were reunited to the joy of both. A note in *The Times* in January 2022 announced the death of Christian's original owner, with a picture of Christian in the back of his car.

This was the era of punk; aficionados wore white knee-high boots, the miniest of skirts, brightly coloured hair, long for men, very short for girls. Their opponents were the skinheads, with shaved heads and Doc Martens boots.

Vivienne Westwood's Shop

The Rocky Horror Show was on, first at the Classic Cinema on the corner of Old Church Street and then at the King's Road Theatre, and the shops catered for all the new trends in fashion, furnishings and entertainment. Some of the great modern clothes designers started their working lives in Chelsea, where they knew that their customers – usually young and forward-looking – would find them. One was Vivienne Westwood. She had a shop at World's End, the further stretch of the King's Road, where the road 'kinked' before reaching Fulham. She changed the fascia from time to time, becoming 'SEX' and later 'World's End'. On the front was a large clock with thirteen figures which rotated backwards. The youngsters mobbed Chelsea on Saturdays, carrying loud music players – ghetto blasters - at full volume. One weekend a rumour arose that there was going to be a street riot between the punks and the skinheads. Some shops even boarded up their windows – we didn't – but although there were many from both sides running about shouting and singing, and a greater than usual police presence, it all seemed reasonably good humoured and no damage was done.

5. King's Road Neighbours

Our parade of shops on the south side, stretching from Paultons Square to Beaufort Street, was a little commune on its own. The shopkeepers were friendly and helpful, though some were slightly eccentric. We were all happy to take in parcels, provide loose change or supply a little milk or sugar. An atmosphere of innocent curiosity prevailed, exchanging gossip and rumour without resorting to malicious small talk. Next to us, towards Beaufort Street, when we arrived, was an antique shop owned by William Bray, always known as Bill. Gruff and uncommunicative until you got to know him, and a confirmed chain-smoker, he was a pleasant neighbour and always gave us first refusal on any books he acquired with his purchases. He had endless stories about his past. He claimed to have been an officer in the Royal Navy, a cowboy in Australia, and several other professions, until he went into the antique business. He sold junk rather than antiques, and his shop was as scruffy as its owner, but every now and again he would offer something valuable and expensive. He didn't stay in the King's Road very long after we arrived – he must have been at least eighty when we came – and was replaced by Stephen King's menswear shop.

Stephen sold highly-coloured Hawaiian shirts. A friend bought one for Leo on his birthday but as far as I know he never wore it, being more of a pipe and pullover man. Some of the shops were really half-shops, with very small spaces. One of these, beside Stephen's, was a small hairdressing salon owned by the German Schumi brothers. Gregor did my hair for some years, eventually leaving the King's Road for a salon in Britten Street. Heinz, a first-class hair stylist, was also an artist, producing huge brightly-coloured abstract canvases which he kept in the salon to the delight (or horror) of his clients.

Another half-shop was the print and bookshop of Martin Orskey, with a curved glass window. He was well-known in the trade and much respected. O.F. Snelling, in his book *Rare Books and Rarer People*, published in 1982, described him as the 'prince of all the book runners – for this is what he was to begin with, and he would be the first to admit it.' His first job was with the book auctioneers Hodgsons, of Chancery Lane, going round the bookshops of London and elsewhere in his spare time. He had an amazing ability to sniff out a bargain, and when he died in his nineties his collection was sold at auction for something just short of a million pounds. Although we must have seemed in competition to Martin, he was never anything but friendly and helpful to us, novices as we were. Further along the parade was Asterix, a restaurant specialising in delicious galettes, pancakes stuffed with every imaginable filling. We discouraged our visitors from bringing them into the shop, to prevent sticky fingers from touching the books., but that didn't stop us from buying them for ourselves.

Early one morning in 1983 a new neighbour arrived in King's Road, a few doors away from us. The empty shop had intrigued us for some time. Some beautiful glass fittings appeared in the windows, the name Rococo was on the fascia, but we had no idea what was to be sold there. That first morning an attractive young woman arrived on the doorstep of the new shop, but seemed unable to get the door open. As we were the only shop open at that hour she asked for our help. We offered her some coffee – our usual reaction to meeting a new friend – and she introduced herself. Her name was Chantal Coady and she was about to open a chocolate shop. Leo followed her back to 'Rococo' and managed to turn the key in the lock. In return he was offered the very first chocolate ever to leave the new establishment, which was later to become a world-renowned source of delicious confectionery. We were able to find from a colleague an early 1890 catalogue – *Letang Fils Paris, Chocolate, Ice Cream Molds* – full of sketches of chocolate designs which Chantal bought and reproduced in blue on white paper to use for the delicate wrapping paper for her chocolates.

At the far end of the parade, on the corner of Beaufort Street, was Terry de Havilland's shoe shop, Cobblers to the World. Terry's shoes were fabulous, way-out footwear, and his customers, who came from every corner of the world of entertainment, included David Bowie, Cher, Bette Midler and even Rudolf Nureyev. On the day the shop opened, Terry employed streakers, totally naked young men and women, to run up and down the road, advertising his wares. They certainly attracted considerable attention.

5. King's Road Neighbours

Before Terry arrived the shop had been Thwaites, an old-fashioned menswear shop. Mr. Thwaite, who dressed traditionally in a homburg hat, was always in his shop with his son, selling conventional men's clothing – tweed jackets, woollen cardigans and old-fashioned underwear – very different from the up-to-date goods of his successor.

One shop in our little parade was Crane Arts, a small art gallery, an offshoot of the larger premises, Crane Kalman, in Brompton Road. The main gallery was established by Andras Kalman, specialising in modern twentieth-century British, European and American art. The King's Road gallery was managed by Tony Ashby, another good friend, who always invited us to his exhibition private views, usually of old and modern naïve paintings. One exhibition was of tiny paintings by Alexander Dunluce, later the Earl of Antrim. For thirty years he was a conservator at the Tate Gallery, and these little oil paintings were executed for his daughter's dolls house. We bought three and I have them still.

There was another half-shop which sold jewellery, owned by Mr and Mrs Gilbert. They were there for some time, but left in very sad circumstances. One afternoon four young men got out of a taxi and asked it to wait. They ran into the shop, forced the Gilberts to the floor behind the counter, grabbed as many brooches, watches and rings as they could and piled back into the taxi. They told the cabbie to drive back to Wandsworth, but someone had taken the number of the cab and they were stopped on Wandsworth Bridge. The poor taxi driver found the police unwilling to believe he was completely innocent. The incident left the Gilberts very shaken, Mr Gilbert was taken ill and they had to give up the shop.

On the other, Paultons Square, side of us was a small dress shop selling young fashions in the latest styles. It was owned by two young women who worked together and lived together, what would later be called an 'item'. They were good fun and would often come into our shop for coffee or a glass of wine. Their shop was called Fruit Fly, which we later learned (we were not very sophisticated then) meant a young woman who hung out with gays. They

Paultons Square

had a beautiful cocker spaniel, nearly always to be found in their shop, and we heard that they were planning for her to have puppies. We put our name down to buy one and waited anxiously for the impending birth. Needless to say the offspring were adorable, some blue roan like their mother, one completely black and two pale cream and white, lemon roans. We decided on one of these, a bitch, and spent as much time as we dared, not in our shop but in the one next door, playing with the puppies. Finally the necessary injections were done and the new arrival, named Tess (of the d'Urbevilles) came to her new owners.

We couldn't leave her at home so she came with us to the shop (our takings improved immediately) and we trained her never to leave the premises without us. On the one occasion I found her outside at the bus stop I was so angry, that she lay on the floor looking at me with her great spaniel eyes, and never did it again. Leo encouraged her to jump up on the chair in front of his desk whenever the local bore appeared, to prevent him being buttonholed for hours on end. Unfortunately she was something of a racist dog, as whenever a black face came in she would bark furiously and had to be severely reprimanded. Even our beloved postman was not exempt.

Other shops on that side of us were Ciancimino, selling beautiful modern Italian furniture, a delicatessen, managed by a Middle Eastern young woman, who, when her boss was out of the shop, stuffed our sandwiches so full of delicious fillings that she would surely have bankrupted him eventually. This was where we usually bought our lunch – CRB didn't close for lunch – eaten in the shop, though if any of us wanted to go out that was fine. Later, after she left Chelsea, another shop with equally tasty sandwiches opened and we continued buying food from the new owner Boris as long as we stayed in the King's Road. With the department store, Peter Jones, not very far away in Sloane Square, it was tempting to disappear for a while at lunchtime. Once Tess was installed there was much competition to walk her round the square, or down to the river.

Philippa with Tess

Another neighbour with a shop in Old Church Street was Manolo Blahnik, whose beautiful shoes are prized all over the world. Manolo came into the shop frequently, sometimes to buy a book perhaps as a present or for himself. Or just for a chat and the inevitable cup of coffee.

Round the corner in Beaufort Street lived the photographer John Bignell. He captured much of Chelsea's exciting high life, published later as *John Bignell, Chelsea Photographer*. His pictures showed some of the distinguished Chelsea residents – and visitors – including Diana Dors and Sammy Davis Jnr, as well as photographs of World's End, Sloane Square, and Chelsea Town Hall. He was a regular visitor to the shop.

One of the best known events of Chelsea was the annual Chelsea Arts Ball, viewed by many as extravagantly shocking. It was held on New Year's Eve, and was originally the brainchild of the Chelsea Arts Club. It now takes place in the Club itself. The Club was founded in 1891 by some of the many artists living and working in Chelsea, and after first finding a home at 181 King's Road, it finally bought a beautiful house in Old Church Street. Under the constitution of the Club two thirds of the Members have to be practising artists, sculptors or designers. Its rules state that 'The Club has no dress code and in truth very few rules; but the few we do have are taken rather seriously. We are an actual not a virtual community. No devices may be used in the Club for any purpose whatsoever'.

CHAPTER 6

Friends in Chelsea (and Elsewhere)

In Paultons Square, a few yards from us along King's Road, lived at one time or another, many distinguished men and women, among them Jean Rhys, Samuel Beckett, Paul Nash and Augustus John, several of whom are commemorated with Blue Plaques. None of these were there in our time. The houses are tall, elegant buildings, some divided into flats but many still in single occupation, each with a good-sized garden. On the far side from us lived the poet Kathleen Raine. We came to know her well as she often visited the shop on her way to the Post Office further down King's Road. She would sit down to have a chat and a rest and sometimes when she had heavy parcels Leo would leave her in the shop while he took the parcels to be posted.

Kathleen was an interesting literary figure, a fine poet and leader of a group of intellectual men and women who published *Temenos*, a 'journal of the imagination'. She liked to talk to Leo about literature, religion and history, and to me about gardening and cats. She had been a close friend of the naturalist and explorer Gavin Maxwell. His book about an otter – *Ring of Bright Water* – took its title from a line in one of her poems. He too had lived in Paultons Square, before our time; unfortunate for us, because he kept a menagerie of animals and birds in the house which I would have loved to

Kathleen Raine

have met, and Kathleen sometimes looked after Mij the otter on the other side of the square.

Kathleen was a close friend of Charles, then Prince of Wales, now King Charles, who would often visit her privately, accompanied only by a single detective. After she died in 2003 I was asked by her daughter, Anna, to undertake the only authorised biography of her, which was published as *No End to Snowdrops* in 2010. I had an interview with Prince Charles who told me about his visits to Kathleen.

Other residents in the Square were the Russell family – father and son Jeremy, both doctors. They had a studio in their back garden which they hired out to budding artists, mostly their patients. Anna, one of our 'girls', was invited to work there and subsequently became a fine painter in watercolours.

A Chelsea friend in the antiquarian book trade was Max Reed, who, in partnership with John Sims, owned a beautiful shop in the Burlington Arcade, later moving to Duke Street, St James's. They dealt in fine books on art and architecture. Max was the son of Sir Carol Reed, the film director, famous for

No End to Snowdrops

such films as *Odd Man Out, The Third Man* and *A Kid for Two Farthings*. He and his wife, Penelope Dudley-Ward, lived further along King's Road. Penelope, a good customer of ours, was the daughter of Freda Dudley-Ward, a former mistress of Edward VIII. Max himself lived at the Old Rectory in Old Church Street, one of the oldest houses in Chelsea, with a large garden, believed to be the second largest in London after that at Buckingham Palace. Our friendship with Max led to our being able to park our car for free in the Old Rectory garden for some years.

Max's half-sister Tracy Reed married the actor Edward Fox, who in a somewhat convoluted association, was to play the Prince of Wales in the television serial *Edward and Wallis Simpson*. Edward's real-life wife, Tracy, was the granddaughter of the Prince's former mistress.

A further addition to the Prince of Wales story was the visit to the shop of the American actress Cynthia Harris, chosen to play Wallis Simpson. She was on her way to talk to the Reed/Fox family, round the corner in Old Church Street, and called in to ask if we had any books on the Abdication story. She was researching the history of the period, and bought two books,

A King's Story by Edward VIII himself, and Frances Donaldson 's *Edward VIII*. We talked for some time and I commented that I thought she bore little resemblance to Wallis. She told me that when she was being dressed for the part, she sat at a dressing table while a black wig was placed on her head, her face was made up carefully over a period of more than an hour, and when she looked in the mirror she was the future Duchess of Windsor.

Once, while our Mini was parked in Max's garden, we asked our current assistant, Anna, to drive it round to the shop, and gave her the key. She returned in a Mini a few minutes later, but it wasn't our Mini she was driving. It was blue not black. Other neighbours used the Old Rectory garden, and this little car belonged to Tony Ashby, of Crane Arts. We never found out how it was that the key fitted both cars.

Another bookseller in Chelsea, in Lawrence Street, though without a shop, was Camille Wolff. This elderly lady (she lived to be 102) was the widow of a lawyer, and specialised in books on true crime. Often known as Mrs Murder, she knew everyone in the book trade and most of her neighbours in Chelsea. She had trained as a doctor, but decided that bookselling was a less responsible job. In fact she had been interested at one time in buying our shop but decided she was not cut out for shopkeeping and preferred to work from home.

Gradually Chelsea Rare Books, now under our control, was becoming a feature of the Chelsea scene. It was the go-to place for anyone wanting a quiet sanctuary for a short while, to sit in a pleasant room, read for a few minutes, or talk to a friendly face. One such who was a regular visitor on Saturday afternoons was an elderly Scottish baron, Lord Kinnaird, father of Anna, one of our assistants. When in London he lived in a flat further along King's Road, and loved to wander through Chelsea, ending up at the shop where he could rest for a while before returning home for tea. He was always immaculately dressed in a camel hair coat, polished shoes and a walking stick, and wore a monocle. He reminded me of P.G. Wodehouse's Lord Emsworth. His journey to the shop provoked from him irascible outbursts against

6. Friends in Chelsea

R.B. Kitaj

modern youth – skirts were too short and hair was too long – but he loved sitting in an armchair, watching the customers, and always asked what they had bought. We were very fond of him, and when we went on a book-buying trip in Scotland, he invited us to tea at the castle.

Across the road in The Vale lived the artist R.B. Kitaj – his first name was Ronald but he was always known as Kitaj. He came into the shop quite often, buying books on art. He had the curious habit of tearing out pictures from these books, scattering them over his studio floor, perhaps to become familiar with the work of earlier artists. One Saturday morning he came in, waited until the shop was empty, then quietly explained to Leo that he wanted to get married (he had been married before) in a Jewish ceremony. He had chosen the oldest synagogue in London, Bevis Marks, for the wedding and Leo told him what might be necessary for the event. On the day of the wedding some of the best-known painters of the time were present; David Hockney was best man, and among the guests were Frank Auerbach, Lucien Freud and Leon Kossoff. Kitaj later painted a picture of the wedding at which all these guests were recognisable.

Kitaj was not afraid to be controversial, particularly where critics were concerned. In 1994 an exhibition of his works at the Tate was universally slammed by the critics and he replied in a violent denunciation of London's art establishment. His wife Sandra Fisher died of cancer shortly after, as a result of this, Kitaj maintained. They had a son Max, and the morning after the child was born Kitaj came into the shop to show us a sketch he had made when the baby was one hour old. Kitaj returned to America after Sandra's death, where he took his own life in 2007.

Another Paultons Square resident who often visited the shop was Lord Slim, son of Viscount Slim of Burma. John Slim was a courteous, friendly customer, who liked to talk to Leo about the war. He bought books on military themes and often reminisced about his father, whose distinguished war record led to his later being appointed Governor-General of Australia.

We were once visited by Princess Margaret. This may have been because her lady-in-waiting, Juliet Townsend, was married to a fellow bookseller with a shop in Brackley. Lady Juliet, the granddaughter of the distinguished barrister and lst Lord Birkenhead, F.E. Smith, was Lord Lieutenant of Northamptonshire, the first woman so to serve. The Princess bought a book or two and I was asked to take them up to Kensington Palace. I was surprised to be allowed to drive straight in, unquestioned, to leave the parcel at the door. Security was much more relaxed in London at that time. I once delivered a book to someone working in the British Library (then a part of the British Museum). I drove straight in through the iron gates and no-one was the slightest bit interested in any credentials. I could have had high explosives in the boot of the car.

Another member of the Royal Family who visited the shop was the Duke of Kent, asking for a present for his wife, who loved cats. We had no books that fitted the bill, but we had bought a small collection of etchings of cats by the Japanese artist Foujita. One of these was the right answer.

A searcher after cat books – and a regular customer – was the distinguished actor Leonard Rossiter. Well known for his television roles as Rigby in *Rising Damp* and as *Reginald Perrin*, he also delighted viewers when, with Joan Collins, he advertised Cinzano, spilling his drink down her dress!

6. Friends in Chelsea

The shop, a visitor once said, smelt of strong coffee and old leather – which we took as a compliment. Coffee (or tea) was always available, real coffee, no instant coffee for us. But when we had been established for a few years, we became a little more adventurous on Saturdays. We employed a series of 'Saturday girls' as most of our regulars were not keen on working at the weekend. Most frequently twins, Jane and Elizabeth, took it in turns to come in on Saturdays – their father was a High Court judge and their brother a distinguished landscape gardener so we knew we were in good hands, and they were always willing to fetch and carry as well as to serve the customers. Not all our Saturday helpers were girls, for one young man, Dickon, at the age of about thirteen loved to come in to help out, running errands, carrying books and wrapping parcels. His sister Emma was another helper, both recommended by Robin de Beaumont, who knew their mother. At lunchtime we offered customers, friends, neighbours and even strangers, a glass of wine and a sandwich or two. We bought the wine across the road from our Pakistani friends and the sandwiches from Boris. The wine, in rather elegant frozen-glass bottles, was pretty undrinkable – Frascati perhaps at £2 a bottle – but it was a convivial hour or two, whether we sold any books or not.

The CRB Christmas parties were also well-known and very well attended. On an evening a few days before the holiday we shut the shop promptly at six. Downstairs in the Beaufort Gallery, in the side room, we had a little Belling electric cooker, where we could heat up soup or lunchtime snacks. For the party we made tiny Welsh rarebits, sausage rolls or vol-au-vents, all home-made by the girls and me. We served small sandwiches, mince pies and apple turnovers. We sent out invitations. Few people bothered to reply but turned up anyway, some without invitations. The wine flowed freely and customers, booksellers, local friends and family always enjoyed the evening.

We made many good friends in the antiquarian book trade. The majority of booksellers were generous with their knowledge and ready to help. I found them very like gardeners, glad to find others with similar interests and full of suggestions, exchanging tips and explanations – perhaps both professions were in it less for the money than for the sheer enjoyment they gained from their work. For that reason it was not unusual to find bookshops gathered together, in one area, seldom competitive and usually willing to recommend others if they could not satisfy their customers' wishes. When we came on to the scene the bookshops were beginning to move away from Charing Cross Road towards Bloomsbury, where some had been for many years. Rents were cheaper, the British Museum was a draw for tourists, and the shops were quaint and old-fashioned, which was attractive to customers young and old.

One of the more unusual bookshops with a central location was Heywood Hill, in Curzon Street. The shop had a long and interesting history. It was opened in 1936 by Heywood Hill himself, succeeded later by Handasyde Buchanan and, in our time, by John Saumarez Smith. Nancy Mitford worked there during part of the Second World War. The shop sold new books as well as second hand, and had a sophisticated atmosphere.

The first 'book town', Hay-on-Wye, was founded by Richard Booth, the 'King' of Hay. It was full of bookshops, and was later followed by the Hay Literary Festival, and by other 'book towns' across the country. We did spend a few days in Ross nearby as a holiday, watching the salmon leaping in the Wye river, but didn't buy any books.

Chelsea and Fulham were also attractive to visitors to London with its share of reasonable hotels, a mixture of shops to suit all tastes, and a long history, with the river Thames an attraction of its own. It was not unusual to walk along the King's Road for half-an-hour or so and not hear a word of English spoken. In the shop we could manage foreign visitors very well. I spoke good French, we had a little German and a few words of Italian, but when it came to visitors from Japan, say, or Romania, we were stumped. It seldom mattered – our customers wanted English books or local prints and we usually got by.

CHAPTER 7

Book Buying

We were often asked how we came by such a comprehensive and often unusual stock of books. A high street shop in such a prosperous, fashionable area as Chelsea often gave us a useful lead over our rival booksellers. After a few years we became a feature of the neighbourhood, open early in the morning for six days a week (in spite of the notice on the door) and known to be friendly and honest. We were the place for people wanting to dispose of any books, from good quality paperbacks to valuable first editions, a single volume or a whole library.

Hardly a day passed without some sort of offer, perhaps a collection of children's books outgrown by their owners, or the library of a departed academic. One problem which often arose in such circumstances was the condition of the books offered for sale. We had to explain that 'Just because it's old, it doesn't mean it's necessarily valuable.' Children are not known for the care they take of their books, and professors acquire their libraries for the contents, not the covers.

Nevertheless, we soon became recognized for paying a fair price for what we bought, often to the surprise of the seller. On one occasion the local dustcart stopped outside the shop. One of the men hopped down and put his head round the door. Leo beckoned him in, wondering if perhaps we were in trouble for not putting our bin outside on time. But the dustman had a book in his hand. 'Have a look at this, will you,' he said. 'Is it worth anything?' The book was well bound in navy cloth and clean, in spite of the hand that held it. 'It fell out of a bin round the corner, and it seems a shame to tip it in the cart.' Leo looked at it carefully. It was a book about ship building, and he asked the man to come back when they had finished their round. We spent the next half hour researching, and discovered that it was an early book on submarines, published in 1918, by the American pioneer, Simon Lake. When our friend returned he was bowled over to be offered £20, a good sum in those days. We sold it to an American collector for a very reasonable profit.

We could never tell where the next purchase would come from. An elderly well-dressed lady came in and explained that her husband, a General, had recently died and she wished to sell his collection of military books. This was a good subject, especially as she mentioned that some of the books were early and all were in good condition. She lived nearby and Leo offered to return with her to view the books. They were indeed well worth a good price, so Leo listed them and came back to go through the list. He telephoned the General's widow and made his offer. To his surprise she said she would have to consult the General before she could agree. The General must have told her to go ahead because she phoned back to say she was happy with the price. Never before or since did we buy books from beyond the grave.

Among the books we were invited to buy by a visitor to the shop was a single small volume of the works of Alexander Pope. It was brought in by a middle-aged man with a slight Irish accent. It was Volume VII of a ten-volume set of Pope's works, in a handsome original calf binding in excellent condition, and dated 1751. We explained that it was only one volume of the set – a fact which he didn't seem to understand – and asked him where he got it from. Perhaps he had the other volumes? No, he said, it came from his granny. This dubious source was that of several books offered to us from time to time. I often wondered if there was a little tribe of 'grannies' offering books for sale. The man agreed to leave it with us while we considered it and to return later.

While he was away we phoned several London booksellers to see if they had missed one volume from an early set of Pope's works, but no-one claimed it. On the seller's return we agreed a small sum for the single volume and he departed happily. We put the book away with some other odd volumes.

About a year later I was browsing through an auction catalogue when Lot 121 caught my eye: a set of ten volumes of the works of Alexander Pope dated 1751, *lacking Volume VII*! It couldn't be, could it? But it was. We viewed the sale and the set was indeed identical to our volume VII. Of course we bought it for a very reasonable sum, to the surprise of our fellow booksellers, and later sold the whole set, now complete, for a very large price. Our mysterious seller was never seen again.

Many were the strange situations and visits we made in search of books. We were excited to be offered some books from Charles Darwin's library. The majority of the valuable volumes had gone to auction but the bulk of the more ordinary books, some signed by him, had lingered in his famous home – Down House – near Orpington, now a museum. The books on offer were in the possession of a neighbour whose family had been friendly with the Darwins and now wished to sell them. We duly arrived and knocked on the front door of the more modest villa nearby. The door was opened by a maid in apron and cap, something which I didn't know still existed. Leo introduced us and said that we had come to look at the books. A haughty voice called out, 'Tell them to come round to the back door. I'm playing bridge.' Obviously we were considered 'trade', and knowing our place we duly backed off and went round to the back door. We did buy the books.

The families of some of Chelsea's distinguished residents frequently offered us small libraries inherited from their famous relatives. Sir Michael Redgrave, with his wife the actress Rachel Kempson, lived in Paultons Square. They had three children, all noted actors, Vanessa, Corin and Lynn. When Sir Michael died we were invited to walk round to see if there was anything we might wish to buy. It was a good collection, though not in brilliant condition. This didn't matter too much because of the provenance. Many were given to the family by other members of the acting profession, often signed by the author or by the donor, and we were pleased to have them, though a little puzzled perhaps that the family should wish to sell. We negotiated a good price and took them back to the shop.

A short time later Corin Redgrave came into the shop, rather angry. Apparently he had not realised that his mother and sisters were selling some of his father's books. The situation was rather tense and we felt ourselves to be in danger of being vilified in Chelsea, sued or even assaulted. But Leo – ever the peace-maker – managed to calm things down and offered to return the books (some had already been sold). Corin huffed and puffed and finally went back to Paultons Square to his family. He returned a few days later with his wife the actress Kika Markham. They were both perfectly charming and we came to a very amicable agreement whereby we kept most of the collection, returning only those which had sentimental value to the Redgraves, and refusing to be compensated for the ones we gave back.

The auction rooms in London (and elsewhere) were a principal source of the books we purchased. Christies (in the West End and at South Kensington), Sothebys (who took over the long-established firm of Hodgsons in Chancery Lane, specialising in book sales), Phillips and Bonhams were the principal auctioneers, but there were smaller rooms – Lots Road in Fulham, Chiswick, Putney and several others in the suburbs. Not all offered books for sale but the major houses held frequent book sales. Most of the West End salesrooms were scrupulous about the way they operated. There were many rumours in the trade (and out of it) about the conduct of the dealers buying at auction. The infamous 'ring' was dying out in London, though it was still operating at some country sales. The lots would be sold at low prices as some dealers refrained from bidding. They would all meet up later in the nearest pub to 'knock down' the lots at a 'private' auction, thus depriving the owners of the lots of an acceptable price, while the winning dealers succeeded in buying up the lots at less than they should have gone for.

We did in fact attend a sale in Suffolk – quite unaware of the operating 'ring'

– and slipped away afterwards with our purchases, delighted with what we had bought. We were later put in the picture by an irate provincial bookseller who thought he had been 'swindled'.

The auctioneers at the sales we attended knew their regular bidders by sight and often by name. On one occasion, when Rachel went to bid on our behalf, she was mistaken by the auctioneer for a member of the staff of Sotheran's, like Rachel, blond, young and pretty. Rachel managed to obtain one lot for us, and the auctioneer called out, 'To Rose of Sotheran's'. 'No,' shouted the furious Rachel, 'To Rachel of Chelsea Rare Books!' She was cheered loudly. Later in our relationship with the auction houses, the bidding method changed. Numbers attached to paddles on handles were issued to bidders when they signed in before the auction. When a lot was knocked down to a customer he would raise his paddle to indicate who he was. This kept the identification of the successful bidder from others in the room, though of course within the trade most were well known to each other. Credit facilities were extended to dealers, and other regular purchasers, provided they kept within the rules – a month's credit was usual – so that they could collect their purchases before they needed to pay and were often able to sell on what they had bought before the due date for payment.

In 1993 the principal auction houses began adding a 'buyer's premium' to the hammer price paid at sales. This was much resented by the trade and by private buyers. The houses claimed this was to cover their costs; the premium was originally 15% and subject to VAT but this was later raised to 20%, though on larger bids (over £10,000) it was less.

It was quite common for auction houses to 'lot up' books sent for sale. Volumes of considerable value were lotted separately, but it was not unknown for multiple lots to contain real bargains, and dealers went to considerable lengths to disguise the fact that they had spotted something special in a job lot. Viewing the lots before the sale carried considerable responsibility, and it was a tribute to a staff member of a bookshop to be allowed to view an important sale. This was more often the duty of the shop owner or dealer himself. The viewer had to assure himself that illustrated books contained the requisite number of plates, that the condition was as good, or better, than the catalogue description and that the edition was exactly what it purported to be.

There were several categories of books which were important to us and which we were always glad to buy. One was Private Press Books. In his book, *The Private Press*, Roderick Cave defined the Private Press as 'presses owned or operated by amateurs who have worked outside the conventional book trade channels'. He went on to explain that in recent years a more commercial outlook by these 'amateurs' grew up, until the output of their presses commanded very high prices and they themselves – artists, engravers, designers and typographers – came to be regarded as the greatest exponents of their trade. The beauty of the print, the illustration, the technical perfection and the binding of these handsome volumes attracted wealthy men of taste, who could appreciate the fine hand-made paper, woodcut initials and engraved borders. They certainly attracted us. As ever condition was vital. The books, often bound in vellum, calf or Morocco with gold tooling, were a pleasure to handle. Many were cloth bound in handsomely designed covers, often with a transparent wrapper to protect the boards. The great Private Presses – Kelmscott, Ashendene, or Doves Press for example – were relevant to the socialism of the late nineteenth century. We liked to believe that our position in south-west London, not far from William Morris's home in Hammersmith, near that of T. Cobden-Sanderson and C.R. Ashbee, with the Vale Press opposite us in Chelsea, gave us a unique insight into the world of fine printing.

Another speciality was early children's and illustrated books. Those heavy quarto volumes, illustrated by Arthur Rackham, Edmund Dulac or Kay Nielsen, commanded high prices. But they were often too cumbersome for the children to read themselves. They needed something more like the Winnie-the-Pooh books by A.A. Milne, or the tiny volumes of Beatrix Potter, not easy to find in good condition after small fingers have turned the pages. We had to learn exactly the requirements for a first edition: dated or

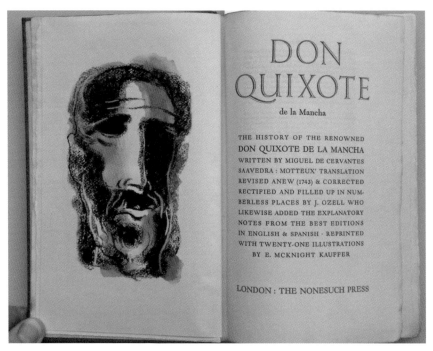

Don Quixote, Nonesuch Press, 1930, Illustrated by E. McKnight Kauffer

Don Quixote and Sancha Panza, ink and wash by Edward Ardizzone

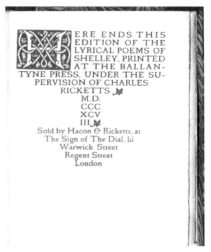

The Lyrical Poems of Shelley. The Ballantyne Press, 1898.

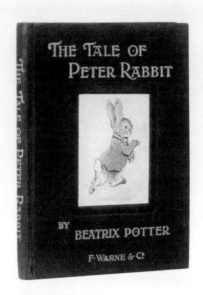

The Tale of Peter Rabbit

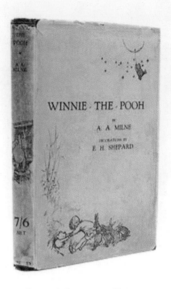

Winnie the Pooh, by A.A. Milne, 1926, 1st edition

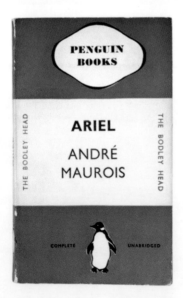

Ariel, The Life of Shelley, Andre Maurois, 1935, the first Penguin

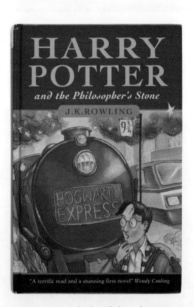

Harry Potter and The Philosopher's Stone, J.K.Rowling, 1997, 1st edition

The Gutenberg Bible, 1455

The Kelmscott Chaucer, 1896

English Madrigals – In the Time of Shakespeare, [1899] bound by Ramage

undated, with coloured endpapers, publisher's name changed slightly. How many would-be sellers did we disappoint when they claimed a first edition and it wasn't.

One book which we would always buy whenever it appeared at auction, usually for a four-figure sum, was *Bits of Old Chelsea*, which contained forty-one etched plates on india paper, each signed by the artist, Walter Burgess. It was published in 1893 as a large folio, bound in red buckram; only one hundred copies were printed and even if one or two etchings were missing we knew that the beautiful black and white plates would sell individually for a handsome sum. Some twenty or more copies must have passed through our hands.

CHAPTER 8

The Beaufort Gallery

When we took over the shop the basement, reached by rickety wooden stairs, was no more than a storage room. It seemed sad to waste such space when we could use it to our advantage. I was interested in antique maps and we both liked watercolour paintings and prints of all kinds. After a couple of years at the shop we decided to turn the space into a gallery for such illustrated materials, together with additional shelf space for a rapidly growing collection of art books. We also had in mind that we might use the Gallery, when it was finished, for exhibition space, perhaps for young artists for a modest fee if we liked their work.

We needed to rebuild the downstairs rooms completely, consisting of the main area from the stairs to the front of the shop, and a small room off it which could still be used for storage. The whole basement was badly lit and the stone flooring needed to be covered. A new staircase, with banisters, was essential, so were better lighting and heating, shelving for books and better facilities for hanging framed pictures. Our next-door neighbour at home was an architect and we asked him if he would undertake the complete renovation of the new gallery. He gladly agreed and came down one Sunday to inspect the premises.

It turned out to be more expensive than we had imagined, but we decided to go ahead hoping that the outlay would be justified. The bank was helpful with a small overdraft, the manager insisting on coming over to see what we were doing. Our architect neighbour designed a handsome staircase, as wide as was possible, with polished handrails and elegant steps. Shelving for the books was no problem, though the space between the shelves had to allow for quarto and folio sized books, usual with books on art and architecture. For the prints we put up shelving with a two-inch wooden lip in front so that we could balance stacks of mounted prints.

For the framed pictures we erected ready-made commercial screens covered in tan hessian, set up around the room, with a space above the print shelves for additional prints, maps and watercolours. We also purchased two or three folding floor stands for larger unframed material.

By the time we had finished the whole gallery looked very attractive, well-lit, bright and welcoming. We placed a large pine table in the centre with a couple of chairs, to encourage customers to browse before buying. The final touch was a large convex mirror, strategically placed by the stairs, so that we could see what was happening wherever we were in the shop. We called the new addition to the shop The Beaufort Gallery and put up a sign outside to show that we were open for business.

Although we were against removing plates from books that were still in good shape, we did often purchase volumes with prints missing, or in poor condition, so we were able to benefit from books that were almost unsaleable as they were, but which contained, say, highly desirable early prints of London, especially Chelsea, views of other countries, sports, animals, flowers and many, many more. An amateur artist friend turned out to be a very skilful colourist and tackled hundreds of prints for us (always labelled 'later colouring'). We found a picture framer further down King's Road who gave us excellent discounts for mounting and framing, and before long we were able to offer a comprehensive stock of all sorts of illustrated material at reasonable prices.

The Beaufort Gallery

The question of antique maps was more difficult. The work of early cartographers, such as Speed, Saxton or Hondius, were much in demand and very expensive. We were seldom able to buy atlases containing such maps and had to reply on the auction houses for the occasional purchase, or perhaps have a lucky find from a private source. But like the prints, there was always the possibility of an incomplete set from a battered book. I needed to do some serious study into map-making (and map selling) to avoid mistakes. Cartography is a very specialised subject, and I learned a great deal from some of the established map-sellers who were always pleased to share their knowledge and experience.

Watercolours too were complicated. We could never claim to be experts, but our own collection and visits to sales (helped by our friends Cyril and Shirley Fry) were a good standby. These delicate English paintings were very popular at the time, and we bought them, nearly always in the minor salesrooms, framed or reframed them when necessary, and found a ready market both from our windows and in the Gallery. We devoted one of our

Old Church Street, Chelsea, etching by Walter Burgess, 1894

8. The Beaufort Gallery

Musicians in a Polar Night, Neville Sattentau

two windows to material from the Gallery, which always attracted attention and often preceded a sale.

Our first exhibition in the gallery in 1975 was of the paintings of a young artist called Neville Sattentau. He had been a painter of miniatures and brought some of them in to show us. He explained that he used an egg tempera technique which gave his pictures an unusual luminosity. We liked the work and as Neville was also interested in book illustration we felt that we might both do well if we offered him the opportunity of an exhibition. He was only too happy for his pictures to be shown and the exhibition was organised by the art critic David Sylvester. It did very well and most of the pictures were sold.

Neville's interest in books led to commissions for him from J.P. Getty, then living in Chelsea. One was *Kubla Khan* by Coleridge, sixteen pages on vellum, and *The Pardoner's Tale* by Chaucer, seven pages on vellum and others, all now in Getty's Library in Oxfordshire. We held several later exhibitions in the Gallery, sometimes of works by single artists, or of collections of etchings, or paintings of Chelsea, but the sales we made of our collections of prints, paintings and antique maps were a very useful addition to the income of the shop.

One of the problems with the Gallery, in spite of the mirror on the stairs, was theft. The unframed material was light to carry and fitted easily into a carrier bag. We asked visitors to leave bags upstairs before they went down to the Gallery, but it wasn't always possible to keep an eye on them when we were busy, and the more professional thieves could secrete small items under their coats, or even in pockets made for the purpose. It was not uncommon for us to go downstairs and find gaps on the walls, or items missing from the collection. Framed pictures were more difficult to 'lose' but it did happen from time to time.

CHAPTER 9

Runners and Rovers

Some booksellers do not operate from a shop. Before the days of the internet it was common practice for 'runners' to buy books from one shop and sell to another. They spent whole days 'on the road', wearing out shoe leather to make a modest living in the book trade. Most were regular visitors and the shop owners knew them well. Lugging enormously heavy loads, in suitcases or rucksacks, they welcomed a brief rest and a cup of tea, knowledgeable about their stock and often specialising in one sort of book or another.

One elderly gentleman, Arthur Howlett, was a favourite of ours. He came to the shop two or three times a month, arriving early when he knew we were open, off the bus from Victoria Station. He never took off his hat, though extremely courteous in an old-fashioned way, and although we always offered tea or coffee, he never accepted. He would suggest he had something 'on board' for us, which was usually a good purchase, and quite often he would buy something from us for his next 'port of call'. I wondered if he had been a seaman at some time. He carried his stock in old cardboard boxes usually falling to pieces, but would never let us offer him a stronger one. Bill Lent of Maggs changed his box for him once, to which Howlett took such offence that he didn't come into them for two years. Only the most sensitive

Baedeker

books were to be wrapped before being added to the day's stock. As for our anxieties about the weight of his cargo – had he not 'run' the twenty-seven volumes of the Nonesuch Dickens in the 1950s?

We learned much from him about books and bookselling and he had intriguing tales to tell. He never said a derogatory word about any bookseller, was always known as 'Mr Howlett', and remained, as long as we knew him, one of the great personalities of the trade.

Another runner, known to all booksellers, was Andrew Henderson. Tall and gaunt, he specialised in books on art and architecture. He had himself been to art school and was something of a painter, but he would never show his work to anyone. His knowledge of the world of art (and of books) was astonishing, as was his memory. He could recall almost every book he had ever sold or bought, and many that he hadn't. He was a man of great integrity, though eccentric in his ways. He lived with his mother in the suburbs, never learned to drive a car or use a typewriter, let alone a computer. In spite of his being a good friend of Chelsea Rare Books, we never managed to feel close to him, nor could we find out what happened to him after we had left the shop.

9. Runners and Rovers

Some of these 'runners' were really 'rovers'. They might buy an occasional book, if they found a cheap bargain and sell it on again later if they found someone who wanted it. One of these was 'young Bernard'. He couldn't have been older than twelve when he first visited us. He collected, for himself or for resale, old copies of Baedeker, the early tourist guides, some of which were rare and valuable. He knew exactly which printing or which edition was worth money and was very meticulous about condition. The variety of bindings, though always in red limp cloth, with marbled edges, were intriguing. We kept unusual 'Baedekers' for Bernard, though he knew far more about them than we did. He would carefully check that all maps and plans were present, and knew exactly the value of each copy. Gradually Bernard moved into a more general interest in second-hand books – he once asked Leo if 'literature is any good' - and went into business on his own. He is now one of the leading antiquarian booksellers in the world, with a fine shop in the West End, and buying and selling on an international scale.

Runners were very competitive, chasing each other round the shops if a whisper of a big new purchase was suspected. We were told of one who found an early James Bond book in a box outside a shop (not ours). He paid a few pence for it, but was noticed by another runner, who took one look and offered £200. Before leaving the shop the first runner had made a very good profit, which was nothing to that made by the second, when he contacted his eager customer and resold it for £2,000.

Some runners had an 'alternative' life style or were known for other reasons than their bookselling activities. Sarah Baddiel, the mother of the comedian and writer, David Baddiel, was a specialist runner in books on golf, and a well-known writer on the subject. Others were actors or authors or even professional men such as accountants and solicitors.

We were rather fond of a young blond American girl, Carol, who cycled up and down King's Road on an ancient bicycle. She bought and sold a few books from time to time, and had married an elderly, very wealthy man, whom no one ever seemed to have met. Her greeting as she swept past, even if the shop door was closed, was always 'Hi, Leo' never waiting for an answer. In private we referred to her as 'cutie pie'.

Another bookseller who started his London bookselling life as a runner was Angus O'Neill. He had an unbelievable memory for books, authors, music, bibliographical detail and many, many other subjects. He had lived with his family in Oxford, gone to Cambridge University and helped out in bookshops from time to time. His mother was a professional pianist and a considerable artist. Angus became a close friend, and when on one of his many journeys around Europe he bought an enormous collection – 28,000 books – which 'completely filled a large flat', he brought them back to Chelsea Rare Books. Gradually he filtered them out into those he knew he could place immediately and those which would take some time to sell. To place them we rearranged our shop shelves, turning them to protrude from the wall instead of flat against it, which gave us far more shelf space, and the whole process was mutually beneficial. Eventually Angus took a shop in Cecil Court but we have remained good friends ever since.

We had many contacts in the trade in this country, in Europe and in America. Neither Leo nor I had ever been to the United States of America, but many friends there had begged us to cross the Atlantic and sample the delights of bookselling over there. On the west coast in particular were some of the greatest antiquarian bookstores in the world. The booksellers bought books from us on their frequent visits to London, and on one occasion, perhaps slightly drunk, we accepted an invitation to a 'book meet' in Los Angeles.

On 8th April 1979, we flew from Heathrow across the Pole to San Francisco, so that we could have a few days there and see the city. We explored on foot, to the horror of some of our American friends, visiting the usual tourists spots, Fisherman's Wharf, the tram cars, Alcatraz and Napa Valley as well as some of the elegant, well-stocked bookshops. Then we hired a car to drive south on the Pacific Coast Highway, via Carmel to Los Angeles. We watched the sea otters lying on their backs to smash clam shells and thought of John Steinbeck, promising ourselves to read all his novels again.

9. Runners and Rovers

In Los Angeles we wandered round the famous sites, marvelling at the shops on Sunset Boulevard, looking up at the Hollywood sign in the hills and visiting the Hall of Fame. The 'book meet' was held in Pasadena, not unlike a Book Fair, and was followed by the best hamburgers we had ever eaten. Finally we flew to Chicago to visit friends, over the Grand Canyon and the desert lands to see in the shortest possible time a little of what we were assured was the greatest city in the world.

It was a remarkable trip lasting nearly three weeks in all, finding new friends and renewing old friendships. We found them all generous and warm and enjoyed new experiences, strange food, unusual shops and a different way of life.

While we were away we left the shop in charge of Anna, our auburn-haired assistant at the time. We hesitated to impose on her the responsibility of managing alone, so she invited a friend, Sam, to join her and together they managed very well. One slight problem was that our custom of offering a discount of ten per cent to trade buyers and regular customers slightly misfired. Anna seemed to think that ten per cent meant £10 off a sale. This was all very well if the sale amounted to £100 or more, but if it was only £15 that didn't leave much for us. However, the two of them coped well, there were no major disasters and we were sure that some customers came in just to see two such handsome young people in charge.

A Chelsea visitor, who seldom bought a book, was Bill Figg. He came from an old Chelsea family and lived in one of the council flats off Beaufort Street. He knew Chelsea well and after retiring (we never learned what he had retired from) he bought himself a camera and wandered round the neighbourhood taking photographs of buildings, gardens and other Chelsea sites of interest.

One day in 1996 he came into the shop carrying a great portfolio full of his pictures and plonked it down on the counter. 'I want to write a book about Chelsea,' he said shyly, 'but I can't write properly. I want you to write it for me!'. The photographs were interesting. Bill was an amateur but he had caught the atmosphere of the place, finding odd angles and unusual corners, using shadows and shafts of sunlight for his pictures that might have been the envy of any professional photographer.

I went through the collection and we worked out a plan to put together a simple booklet using the best pictures, the ones that might appeal to anyone wanting to know a bit about Chelsea without having to plough through a long history, of which there were many about the borough. I then wrote a paragraph or two for each entry. We called it *Hidden Chelsea* and it was agreed that Chelsea Rare Books would publish it and pay for it, selling it in the shop and elsewhere if we could, and Bill would get a royalty on each sale. It was a great success, selling at most bookshops including W.H. Smith. Bill was delighted.

One of our other 'extras' was the provision of book-plates (the 'Ex Libris' labels stuck into a book to show ownership). A local artist, Oriol Bath, was commissioned to design the plates, after meeting the customers at the shop and discussing what might be appropriate. A cat lover, for example, might want a cat design; a book picture was obviously a possibility, flowers, birds, trees or other natural pictures. Oriol seemed able to turn her imagination to any suitable illustration and we had many requests for bespoke book-plates. Other features of the stock, often shown in the window, were wooden book holders, expanding book stands and troughs, many decorated with carvings or illustrations. Most were Victorian – one or two much older – trimmed in brass or silver. Leo's sister Gladys, who loved visiting antique shops and fairs, bought them for us and customers found them useful as presents. We did consider stocking other book furniture, revolving bookcases for instance, but space in the shop did not allow for any larger pieces, so we contented ourselves with smaller table-top book stands.

CHAPTER 10

Safety and Security

There is a limit to what a shopkeeper can do to keep himself, his staff and his stock safe from theft and violence. In the days before CCTV, hidden cameras and intricate alarm systems we had to rely on sharp-eyed assistants and simple locks and keys. Booksellers also tried to keep the shelves full so that any gap would immediately be noticed. Theft from bookshops was rife – there was even a theory that the printed word was for all and books should not be bought or sold! However, this idea was not behind the frequent pilfering of books. They were stolen to be resold and booksellers did their best to hold on to their stock.

The Antiquarian Booksellers Association set up a telephone chain, so that any bookseller who found a gap on his shelf that should not be there could telephone the ABA office and describe the missing book. The office would then phone details through to a few members, who would in turn call a few more until everyone knew of the theft, and would take care not to purchase the book from the thief. This of course could not work completely efficiently when many booksellers were not members of the trade association. However it was a help, and more than once when a bookseller further along King's Road lost a book, the thief walked a few hundred yards down to us and offered it for sale. We had already been forewarned and tried to hold the thief until either the police or the deprived bookseller arrived at our shop. On one occasion the bookseller got to us first, dragged the thief out into the street and set about him with considerable violence. The weedy thief, high on drugs, refused hospital treatment.

Chelsea then was often the centre of unhappy youths, mentally unwell or addicted to drink or drugs. Jane, one of our assistants, and I were alone in the shop one afternoon when a scruffy young man tottered in and took a Stanley knife from the counter. Without thinking I grabbed his arm and in the tones of an elderly schoolteacher, told him to put it down 'at once'. Jane took his other arm, he dropped the knife and we escorted him firmly out of the shop. He was so surprised that he ran off down the road, leaving us shaking and tearful, but sound in wind and limb with the shop stock intact.

After that incident, we installed an alarm bell under the counter, which when pressed would ring in Stephen King's shop next door, Crane Arts and also in Rococo a few doors away. If the bell ever rang everyone in all three shops would rush out into the street to see what was amiss. It only happened once or twice: when Stephen King pressed it by mistake while slightly the worse for wear, and when Leo on his own knocked over a temporary bookcase and couldn't get out from beneath it.

The only major problem that happened to us while we were in Chelsea was an attempted smash-and-grab raid when a window was broken. We were telephoned at home by the police during the night to say that an attempt had been made to break in by throwing a brick through the window. It seems that it was more likely to have been a drunken brawl than a planned burglary, as we were surrounded by occupied flats above us and opposite, and nothing was taken. The street was busy throughout the night, with night buses up and down, pubs and restaurants open late and a police presence patrolling from time to time. Anyway we had to come down to King's Road to make sure that nothing had been stolen and to secure the premises. A kindly policeman was standing guard when we got there, and had already phoned a security firm to get the window boarded up until we could have the glass replaced.

However it was a shock and could easily have been far worse. Our insurance paid for the repairs though our premium went up the following year. We considered installing a burglar alarm but never got around to it, and as it happened never had any more trouble from the street.

In spite of our precautions books were stolen from the shop. We did our best to keep the valuable items either locked in the cupboard or in the more inaccessible corners of the shop, behind Leo's desk or high up on the shelves where steps were needed. When we opened the Beaufort Gallery downstairs risks were increased. Quite often we would need to go downstairs to assist a customer or reshelve items, leaving the upstairs unattended. Of course we were aware of the problems and did our best to cover all areas, but inevitably we lost books from time to time. I don't think there were ever concerted attempts to steal, such as one thief calling us down while another looted the upstairs shelves. When items did go missing it was usually the odd volume disappearing on the spur of the moment. We actually lost more prints from downstairs while a visitor was alone in the basement. Strangely these were almost always the inexpensive mounted prints which could be tucked into an overcoat, though on occasion we did lose a framed watercolour or a map, and there was little we could do to prevent this. We did investigate the possibility of tagging the more expensive items electronically, but the cost was prohibitive. It was cheaper in the long run to put up with the odd theft.

There are frequent thefts of valuable items from shops, libraries and private collections. These are usually widely publicised so that the thief would find it difficult to profit from his crime. One particular problem arises from the theft of valuable maps removed from atlases and sold on as single items. Professional thieves will open an atlas in full view of the owner or librarian, take a damp string or tape and lay it down on the hinge edge of the map. It is then easy – and noiseless – to gently tear out the map and secrete it under a jacket, to be offered later to a dealer for a handsome price. Antique maps are much in demand and it is seldom possible to establish the rightful owner of such an item. Libraries often stamp every map in an atlas so that its origins are obvious, but this greatly devalues the piece if the atlas is later to be sold.

The Art and Antiques Squad at Scotland Yard has done much work in chasing stolen books, listing valuable items in an attempt to reunite them with their owners. Established in 1969, it was dissolved in the mid-1980s, much to the chagrin of those engaged in the trade. After the London bombings of 2005 it was revived; the unit maintains the London Stolen Arts Database containing details of thousands of items of stolen cultural property, but is composed of only six officers (the Italian Carabinieri Art Squad employs around 300 detectives). However at the time of the Grenfell Fire several members of the unit moved to help with the aftermath and the unit is still not up to strength. Several serious thefts from booksellers and libraries have been front-page news, but it is only those of importance which warrant such publicity. The smaller problems faced by booksellers are now helped by the installation of modern methods of detections, such as hidden cameras, which need not involve great expense and are easy to install. Sadly, they were not yet available to us.

CHAPTER 11

Awkward Customers

The old phrase 'The customer is always right' could never be applied to a bookshop. Every single one of our customers could be charming and difficult at the same time. Buying a book is not like buying a pair of trousers or a can of beans. It may be as easy as picking the right book off the shelf, paying for it and walking out. But it often demands considerable time and thought, close attention from the shop owner, and very difficult decisions.

The attention given to a customer can vary from keeping right out of the way and leaving him to decide what he wants, to fussing around with suggestions which may or may not be the answer. The customer might leave the shop empty-handed with the shop table piled high with rejects, sometimes without even a 'thank you'. Or perhaps the ideal book is found at once with generous congratulations and a 'See you again soon.'

A distinguished Member of Parliament, living in Chelsea, came in and bought a considerable number of fine leather-bound books. He paid for them and took them away. Two days later he came back with the books, and with some excuse about his wife not wanting them after all. We returned his cheque, which we hadn't cashed, and thought no more of it, though of course regretting the lost sale. A month or two later the same thing happened – a good sale of fine books only to be brought back later. We again returned the cheque, though this time without a smile. Speaking to an antique dealer along the road, we found that the gentleman was in the habit, when entertaining important guests at home, of 'borrowing' books, furniture, and even rugs for his house, and returning them when his guests had departed. He didn't dare show his face in any such shop again.

Many distinguished names from the worlds of the theatre, parliament, sport and entertainment visited Chelsea Rare Books. Some were there to buy a present, others were collectors or just readers. There was an unspoken rule of honour that we didn't acknowledge or admit recognition of famous faces – they were just booklovers and that is how we treated them. For some of the girls this was difficult. For them the pop world was a wondrous focus of admiration. The band Duran Duran – all of them – came in to buy a present for Yasmin Le Bon, a book collector herself and wife of Simon Le Bon. Jane was somewhat overwhelmed but kept cool and dignified and made a very good sale.

We were both in the shop, with Rachel 1, when a handsome couple visited us, informally dressed and very friendly. I recognised him as I had recently seen the film *Withnail and I*, written and directed by Bruce Robinson. *Withnail and I* was a British black comedy, loosely based on Robinson's life in London in the late 1960s. The plot followed two unemployed actors, Withnail and I – portrayed by Richard E. Grant (it was his first film) and Paul McGann – who share a flat in Camden Town. It became something of a cult classic. With Bruce that day was his long-term girlfriend, Lesley-Anne Downe, a most beautiful girl and a fine actress who had made her name in the television series *Upstairs, Downstairs*, and went on to star in several hit films. The two visited us often after that, becoming, like so many of our customers, good friends.

Another couple from the world of show business were Toyah Willcox and Robert Fripp, both musicians; Toyah later became well known as a serious actress. They enjoyed coming into the shop, feeling perhaps that we welcomed them as friends and customers rather than for their fame in the field of entertainment. When we first knew them they were just a Chelsea 'couple', but in 1986 they married (a lasting marriage) and Robert bought Reddish House in Wiltshire, the former home of Cecil Beaton. He would tell us all about the refurbishment of the house and bought several books for their library.

The maker of Princess Diana's wedding dress, Elizabeth Emanuel, came into the shop. She wanted a birthday present for a friend, 'a man who had everything'. She chose a beautiful copy, bound in vellum, of Wordsworth's *Intimations of Immortality,* an Essex House Press book with illustrations by Walter Crane. The book is now in the Clarence House library.

In those days one could buy leather bound books quite cheaply as decoration or to fill a bookcase. Theatre producers might borrow some for a play set or an interior designer buy a few yards of books for a customer's shelves. One designer insisted only on books bound in blue leather 'to match the curtains'. One distinguished customer was the cardiologist Dr Derek Gibson, a pioneer in the field of echocardiography. He was rather shy, in spite of his achievements, and a man of great taste. He bought books of different kinds, usually slightly unusual in subject matter, ranging from classics and literature in fine bindings to important early scientific works. He was an excellent musician – doctors often are - and told us once of a beautiful harpsichord he had bought. 'I'd love to see it', Leo said and we were immediately invited to his elegant flat on Cheyne Walk overlooking the river. It was a memorable visit. He was a confirmed bachelor and the flat was most handsomely furnished with eighteenth-century English furniture. The harpsichord was a beautiful instrument with the soundboard decorated with a delicate design of flowers, leaves and birds. We felt privileged to see it, enjoying a glass of dry sherry while we talked about books and music and painting.

It was not only their purchases that made our customers interesting. An American visitor was once browsing the shelves when another came in. This

Flora Graeca Title page

11. Awkward Customers

gentleman asked for an important work on American history, which we happened to have. When he mentioned the author's name the first customer turned round. 'Why, that's me!' he called out, 'who are you?' It turned out that these two academics had for years carried on arguments, sometimes quite acrimoniously, without ever actually meeting. We sat them both down and let them talk, now in a very friendly manner. They left the shop together, still chatting away happily. We felt we had played a small part in the furtherance of transatlantic scholarship.

One of our most important customers was a Greek shipping magnate. A sophisticated, well-educated and very wealthy man, he became a good friend. I asked him how it was that he spoke such good English. He explained that he had had an English nanny. Not only that, but he went to Westminster School and then to Magdalen College, Oxford. Always elegantly dressed, he drove a magnificent gun-metal coloured D-type Jaguar with Greek plates, and when in London lived in a fine flat beside the Albert Hall. In Greece he owned an apartment in Athens, as well as an island in the Aegean. In spite of all this he was a quiet, rather modest and highly intelligent man.

His first purchases were usually books on Greek history or English classics, but as he gradually came to know us better he began to add to the considerable library formed by his father. These rare and expensive purchases were mostly works on Greek topics of all kinds and often illustrated with beautiful hand-coloured plates. They included Greek travel, costume and natural history, extending to the history of the Ottoman Empire. Perhaps the most valuable was a complete set of *Flora Graeca*, a work in ten volumes on the plants of Greece, published in the late eighteenth century from a survey by John Sibthorp and Ferdinand Bauer. Each volume contained one hundred plates, each hand-coloured. The set we bought for him at auction was in an original calf binding – one of the most handsome purchases we ever made.

Our Greek customer was friendly (they had been at school and university together) with the son of a distinguished member of parliament, later a peer, who had a large estate in Hampshire. He purchased the stable block of his friend's estate and began to furnish it with the best furniture, rugs and paintings. He examined every London auction catalogue and viewed the lots that appealed to him; we were then entrusted with attending the sales and bidding on his behalf. We took only a modest commission but as the purchases came to many thousands of pounds, we were able to make a considerable amount of money in the process. He paid us promptly, in time for us to settle the bills immediately. We also had to arrange collection of the items, either ourselves if they were small enough, or via a freight company if they needed a furniture van.

When the Hampshire property was ready for occupation, the new owner talked to me about his small courtyard garden. He knew of my interest in gardens and asked if I would like to design one for him. I jumped at the chance and after a visit to Hampshire quoted him a price – which I later realised was far too low. Nevertheless it was a delightful opportunity for me to work on a project very dear to my heart, knowing that money was no object. I planned the small plot carefully, with a little fountain in the centre of circular paving, and a border based on Greek plants found in the *Flora Graeca*. The landscaping was done by the estate workers, and I could afford to indulge in the very best quality plants, to have something in flower all the year round. The garden was a great success and our customer was delighted.

I felt that this was something which might be useful to me if and when we had to give up the shop. I enquired about finding some training in garden design and discovered that the Chelsea Physic Garden in Royal Hospital Road housed The English School of Gardening, offering courses in garden design. Founded by Rosemary Alexander, the School included a year's correspondence course on surveying, site analysis, planning and landscaping, as well as planting plans. It suited me perfectly as I could work from home, visiting the school, round the corner from the shop, whenever it was necessary. I thoroughly enjoyed the course, and did very well in the plant section, though I found the draughtmanship very difficult – I could never really draw a straight line even with a ruler.

CHAPTER 12

Summer in Aldeburgh

In our search for watercolours to sell in the gallery, and for ourselves, we had come to know Shirley and Cyril Fry. The Fry Gallery in Jermyn Street, specialising in eighteenth- and nineteenth-century British watercolours and drawings, was a favourite haunt of ours. Although the Frys stocked some expensive examples of the best work of leading artists, they also managed to find more modest, lesser-known works, several of which I still have.

After his lease was up in 1988 Cyril took on a small shop in Aldeburgh on the Suffolk coast during the time of the summer music festival. This took place at The Maltings in Snape, a village a few miles from the small town. The Aldeburgh Festival of Music and the Arts was founded in 1948 by Benjamin Britten, Peter Pears and the writer and producer Eric Crozier. Imogen Holst, the daughter of the composer, introduced early choral music, and soon works by more modern composers were offered in the programme. Johnny Dankworth and Cleo Laine, Joyce Grenfell, Peggy Ashcroft and actors from the Royal Shakespeare Company made regular appearances; Princess Grace of Monaco came to take part in a poetry recital. Simon Rattle brought his City of Birmingham Symphony Orchestra to Snape. There was a strong connection with Russian music. The cellist Mstislav Rostropovich was a frequent visitor. He turned out to be known in some way to the family of our assistant, Rohays, who came to Aldeburgh with us on occasion.

Peter Pears, in addition to his role as joint Artistic Director, was a regular performer, often accompanied by Benjamin Britten. In 1979, Rostropovich conducted the Britten–Pears School in a performance of Eugene Onegin (with Pears as guest in the role of M. Triquet, and Eric Crozier as the valet Guillot). We were privileged to be there.

We had often visited the town in summer while the festival was on as we had a friend, Constance Stuart, who had a cottage there. Constance was an unusual woman, claiming direct descent from Mary Queen of Scots. Her mother had been a suffragette and she herself was a supporter of the feminist movement, such as it was in those days. She was a qualified accountant working in the City for one of the accountancy giants, the first woman company secretary. She knew the City of London as if it was her own back garden, was something of an expert on wine, and was a close personal friend of many of the great city magnates.

On one of the Frys' visits to the shop, Constance happened to drop in. They knew each other slightly because of the Aldeburgh connection, and Leo mentioned that we hoped to make a short visit there for the forthcoming festival. It was, I think, Cyril's suggestion that we might take some books down to sell there, covering the costs of a pleasant little holiday. 'We have a small inner room at the gallery in the High Street. You could have it if you can put up some shelves and find somewhere to stay.' Before we could accept this generous offer, Constance intervened. 'I have a friend with a big house on the sea front,' she said. 'She lets it in the summer while she is away. She hates Aldeburgh at festival time'.

It turned out that the owner of the house refused to let us pay rent as she liked the house to be cared for while she was not there. Cyril, too, was happy to have his 'inner room' occupied as we could look after the gallery from time to time while he and Shirley were out. It looked as if we might enjoy a profitable and very enjoyable holiday. It was the first of many.

12. Summer in Aldeburgh

Strafford House, Aldeburgh

A week or so before the festival was due to start we went down to Aldeburgh on a 'dummy run' to review the situation. We took with us some of the folding bookcases we used for book fairs and set them up in Cyril's gallery in the High Street. Constance had the keys to our holiday home – Strafford House – and we went to investigate. The house, painted in primrose yellow, was huge; it was on three floors, could sleep about ten people, and was immediately facing the sea across the road. It had wonderful facilities: several bathrooms, a big kitchen and as many mod. cons., including a big fridge and a chest freezer, as one could wish for.

We decided that this was going to be a Chelsea Rare Books summer event. Constance managed to get tickets for most of the best concerts at The Maltings in Snape, and we invited as many friends, family, customers and fellow booksellers as wanted to come. We made up a careful diary so that we knew who would be coming and when, and where they would sleep. On each bedroom door was a pretty sign of an opera (Rigoletto, Carmen, Tosca, etc.), painted by one of our girls. I have kept them all. We filled the freezer with food, the car with petrol and the bookshelves with books. It was explained to all our guests that they could come and go as they pleased. We would not cook or arrange meals for them but they could help themselves to anything they wanted from larder, fridge or freezer. We kept the house unlocked except at night, after people got back from the concerts (latecomers often climbed in through the windows), and asked only that people changed bedlinen when they left, ready for the next arrivals.

This happy arrangement worked very well for the three weeks of the Festival, and was followed by similar visits in subsequent years. This little offspring of the bookshop in Chelsea was busy and we sold books to many of the Festival artists as well as the visitors. Peter Pears came in from time to time and so did many of the distinguished musicians and actors taking part in the Festival. The hotels were nearly all full.

One particular participant, Cathy Berberian, an Armenian/American singer with a great personality and vivacious temperament, who was staying at a hotel along the front, decided that she didn't like the wallpaper in her room. Unfortunately there were no other rooms available in the whole of Aldeburgh. Constance Stuart, always with her ear to the ground, suggested that perhaps we could put her up. We had a good front room unoccupied at that time and offered it to Miss Berberian. She was delighted, particularly as she didn't have to pay for it, and entertained us all royally on the evenings she was not appearing at The Maltings.

CHAPTER 13

A Philippine Invasion

One sunny Saturday afternoon in Chelsea I was standing by the shop door, gazing out at the street. The shop was empty and I watched as a big black car with darkened windows glided past. To my surprise it reached the bend of King's Road just past us, and regardless of the traffic, turned in the road and came back on the other side. Again it slowly passed the shop, executed another three-point turn and came back. It stopped outside the shop and two burly men, dressed all in black, got out. One crossed the road and stood facing us; the other took up a position at our door. A third man, clearly the chauffeur, opened the passenger door. Out stepped a small, soberly-dressed woman who walked into the shop, strode past me without word, and approached Leo, sitting at his desk. He stood up. 'Can I help you?' he said. The woman drew herself up – she was hardly five feet tall – and said in a clipped, Spanish accent, 'My lady wishes to see books.'

Leo retained his composure. 'Please ask her to come in.' We had no idea who 'My Lady' was, clearly not of the English nobility. Then who? The two heavies were obviously body-guards and to my horror I saw them both take handguns out of their pockets as the chauffeur opened the car door. Then I realised who our visitor was. Out of the car stepped an elegant, black-haired woman, beautifully dressed. She swept imperiously into the shop and I

Mme Marcos

recognised her at once: Madame Imelda Marcos, wife of the President of the Philippines.

Leo greeted her as he would any other customer and asked if she was looking for any books in particular. She explained very courteously that she was in the course of building an English library in Manila and needed a good number of books: art, literature, history and 'any other subjects of interest'. She asked his name and proceeded to take a few books from the shelves. She handed each one to her companion who placed them on the tables. When they were fully laden the books were piled on the floor. After a while it was difficult to move around and Leo whispered to me to close and lock the shop. Outside in the street passers-by were curious to know what was going on, nervous of the baleful Philippinos guarding the door.

'Well, Mr. Leo,' Madame continued, 'I am particularly interested in books on art. Do you have such?' He explained that our books on art were down in the basement and she made her way majestically downstairs. After a short while she called to him. 'I take all,' she said, 'All the art.' By now the situation was fraught. How were we going to cope with packing, was her money good? We would soon have an almost empty shop. Remembering the familiar tale about the Marcos shoe collection (she was reputed to have 3,000 pairs), and rumours of her extravagant shopping sprees, we were very nervous.

13. A Philippine Invasion

When Madame finally finished, she explained that there would be a private plane flying to Manila the following day and the books were to be on it. She was staying in a flat in Campden Hill – a very expensive part of London – and in the morning would send cars and men with boxes to pack the books and take them away. She would pay us in cash – a sigh of relief all round – and we were to total up the cost. She opened a magnificent lizard-skin handbag and handed Leo $1,000 in notes on account; we were to go to Campden Hill the following day to collect the remainder. The party then said elaborate farewells and returned to the car. Accompanied by a bottle of wine, it took us until nearly ten o'clock that evening to list and count the books. The total came to a little over £9,000. We arrived home exhausted, not knowing whether to be thrilled by such a sale, depressed by the empty shelves or terrified by the thought of finding an empty flat when we reached Campden Hill the next day .

But all was well. Madame's companion hardly glanced at the account we presented. She handed over the dollar bills and the books were carefully packed and taken away in five large cars. We couldn't bank the cash as it was a Sunday, but Leo slept with it under his pillow that night. When our assistant arrived at the shop on Monday morning, she took one look at the empty shelves thinking we had been burgled, and burst into tears.

—·•·—

For many years, in fact for all the time we had been in the shop, we had felt that we needed some sort of reference book that would answer the questions we met every day. There were plenty of works on bibliography, on book making, on the subjects to which the books were devoted. But for ourselves and for our assistants, we needed something more - a bookselling dictionary, perhaps, when we encountered a term we hadn't met before. Or an explanation of the different methods of illustrating books; how to recognise unsigned early maps; the value of autographed copies. The more we thought about it, the more complex the idea became. The only answer was to compile such a book ourselves. I had approached a publisher I knew, Scolar Press, about another project (to do with bookselling in London) and talking to my

Antiquarian Books – A Companion

contact there I mentioned the new idea. She responded enthusiastically at once and the new baby was conceived. Giving birth was quite another matter.

Our first idea was something like the Oxford Companions – a companion to bookselling perhaps. We sat down with Angus O'Neill – knowing that his memory and experience would be invaluable – to try to thrash out the background to the book. We knew that if we got it right it would appeal to our fellow booksellers and to anyone involved in the day-to-day handling of books. The answer became *Antiquarian Books – A Companion for Booksellers, Librarians and Collectors.* I was to be the General Editor and Leo and Angus responsible for much of the book's shorter pieces. But what made the work reliable and professional was that we decided to enrol experts for the longer articles, men and women whose long experience in their specialised fields made it believable – and saleable.

The book set out to provide in one volume much of the essential information required by those who sell antiquarian and second-hand books and by those who buy them. We noted in the preface that, regarding the specialist articles, 'this weight of knowledge and expertise has not squeezed out the individuality (nor even eccentricity) which characterise the antiquarian book trade.' These articles included Private Press Books, Autographs and Manuscripts, Incunabula, Science and Medicine, Book Auctions, Cookery Books, Computers for Booksellers, and Restoration and Repair, among others, all written by experts in their field.

The shorter pieces, explaining terms, special collections, bibliographical notes, distinguished libraries etc., we dealt with ourselves and the book was fully illustrated. It was at this time that we bought our first computer – an early Amstrad – and I taught myself to use it. Amstrad was founded in 1968 by Alan Sugar at the age of twenty-one. The name is a contraction of Alan Michael Sugar Trading. Niece Rachel was a great help in getting the text online and although Leo never learned to use a computer we were not without one after that.

Though the articles were alphabetical, there was a comprehensive index. The book, a heavy quarto, bound in red buckram with a simple but eye-catching dust wrapper, finally appeared in 1994 and was, to our surprise and delight, a great success. It was bought – at a price much higher than we wished – by most booksellers and many others – and was well reviewed. It went into a second edition the following year, but though it still remains useful is now very out-of-date.

CHAPTER 14

The End of the Story

B y the end of 1999 we became aware that we were approaching the end
of our time in Chelsea. It was clear from talks with other shopkeepers
that rents were rising. Our own lease was nearing its end and we
waited in some trepidation to hear from our landlords. Sure enough when
the letter came the proposed rent was astronomical. We were asked for a rent
increase of close on 200%, a figure which no second-hand bookshop could
manage. In any case we were beginning to feel our age. The boxes of books
seemed to be getting heavier, the journey from home seemed longer every
day and we were feeling tired. Leo's health was worrying me, though he was
very reluctant to entertain the idea of giving up.

I was giving considerable thought to what I could do with my time if we had
no shop. I would of course want to continue in the world of books, but was
also very intrigued by the idea of working in the horticultural field, though
not as a jobbing gardener. I did some research into what was available in
the gardening world that might not only give me some pleasure but would
also bring in a little money. I found that the school at the Chelsea Physic
Garden – one of my favourite haunts while we were in the King's Road – was
highly regarded as a training school in garden design. I contacted the English
School of Gardening. It offered a year's course in garden design, arranged as a

correspondence course, with practical guidance and training in horticulture, plant information and gardening skills of all kinds. It seemed ideal and I signed up for the year's course, starting in the autumn.

If we decided to abandon the shop it would still be possible to deal in books on a small scale, as so many booksellers did, working from home, on the internet – now a part of every dealer's operation – and appearing at as many fairs as we could manage. We could still belong to the ABA, with a change of address, and keep our customer lists. We decided to renew the lease and sell it on to a more affluent proprietor.

We started putting out feelers to find out who might take the shop if we could negotiate the new lease. Several commercial possibilities arose though no booksellers were interested once they knew what the rent was likely to be. Number 313 was in a good position, on a main shopping street, in a prosperous area with excellent transport – it seemed a desirable place to trade. We were contacted by several clothing shops, a toy shop and two restaurants. The most likely taker was an elegant parfumier, with branches across London whose name was well known. The lady proprietor visited several times, was perfectly willing to pay us a good sum for the lease, and we thought we were home and dry. But she found another shop nearer to the 'best' end of King's Road – usually considered to be the Sloane Square end – and changed her mind.

The next approach was from an Italian shoemaker. The owner was very charming, Italian himself, and clearly very enamoured of the area. Apart from Manolo Blahnik in Old Church Street there were no other shoe shops anywhere near us and the high rent didn't seem to worry him. I was not overwhelmed by the Italian charm and was not sure about his financial stability. However both Leo and our estate agent who was handling the deal seemed to think he was in earnest so we went ahead. Papers were drawn up and plans were made. All we needed was the money for the lease.

We decided to continue as Chelsea Rare Books, working from home online.

14. The End of the Story

We told our regular customers of our plans and decided what stock we would take with us. Obviously it was impossible to continue selling our ordinary stock. Most of the books were of little value and depended on visiting customers for sales. So we decided to put them into auction, with a few 'prizes' to sweeten the lots. A friend from one of the auction houses came down to view and we started packing up. As it happened we did well out of the auction and found a print seller who was happy to take the majority of the contents of the Beaufort Gallery. We held a sale of the watercolours and maps which were of no use to us working from home. Finally we carefully packed up the best of the stock ready for selling in our new 'shop'. We also took the folding bookcases and several other bits and pieces from the shop, including two handsome Art Deco flower vases that had belonged to Robin Greer and which I had always liked.

But what of our Italian shoemaker? We had signed the new lease over to him and he signed his part of the arrangement. All we needed was the cheque. It was a long time coming. Leo, always a worrier, was unable to sleep and his yearly visit to the cardiologist was not encouraging. Eventually we opened the shop one morning and there on the doormat was a brown envelope containing the cheque. We hastened across the road to pay it in, fearing it would bounce. But it didn't and we were all set to go. We handed over the keys and refused to visit the shop again, unwilling to see what was done to it. As it happened nothing could be changed outside as it was a listed building, and our home was a long way away, so we seldom happened to be passing.

At home we set up the folding bookcases in the dining room and arranged the books we had taken from the shop. We sent out an email to all our customers, put a small advertisement in our local North London newspaper and the trade press, and sat back to wait for orders. They were few and far between to begin with, but we did have a fair number of phone calls from fellow booksellers and customers, as well as local enquiries, some of which we were able to fulfil at once. The local Post Office soon got to know us as we called in with parcels, but compared with Chelsea business was slow. We did have several offers of books, but on the whole the quality was not as good as we had hoped. It was no longer possible for us to take large quantities of inexpensive books. What we needed was a few fine offers which could be taken to book fairs or sold to customers we knew. Many phone calls resulted in apologies for not being able to buy the books and disgruntled callers who wanted to know what was wrong with their treasured volumes.

Leo's health was not too good and he had to go into hospital for an operation. Sadly his heart couldn't take it and he died in the Royal Free Hospital on 16th September 2003. I thought perhaps I could carry on Chelsea Rare Books on my own, but it was impossible and I quietly let our beloved shop disappear from view. For several years I was contacted with offers of books and requests for special titles. Other booksellers were very helpful, remaining friends and offering assistance where it was needed. The success of *Antiquarian Books* encouraged me to think I might move away from selling books to writing them.

I was contacted by the daughter of Kathleen Raine, our old friend from Paultons Square, to ask if I would undertake a biography of her mother. The research for the book, together with the long and complex writing of a work about a distinguished literary character, took some three years, and was eventually published by Shepheard Walwyn, a small academic publisher.

The success of the book – *No End to Snowdrops, A Biography of Kathleen Raine* – made me realise that I did have a certain facility for words, and several historical works followed. I enjoyed the research, visiting libraries and museums, interviewing those who knew more about a subject than I did. Writing books instead of selling them seemed a natural progression from the days at Chelsea Rare Books. Ideas flowed from the works of the writers whose books had sat on our shelves for all those years. Even mentioning the name of the shop opened the way in to new perceptions. The most recent work, *Mithras to Mormon: A Religious History of London*, introduced worlds hitherto unknown. I visited mosques, cathedrals, synagogues and temples, without once encountering anything but warmth and friendliness and willingness to help. The Foreword was written by the Bishop of London, the Right Reverend Sarah McNally, the first woman to hold the post and the launch of the book in 2018 was at the Charterhouse in the City.

Our years at Chelsea still remain very clear in my mind. Few people are fortunate enough to enjoy every moment of their daily work; on Sunday evenings Leo could hardly wait to return to the shop the following day. Each week, each day, held something new. I will not forget the books – or the customers.